Rules for Living:
The Ethics of Social Cooperation

An Abridgment of
The Foundations of Morality

by Henry Hazlitt

Edited by Bettina Bien Greaves

1999
The Foundation for Economic Education, Inc.
Irvington-on-Hudson, New York

Rules for Living: The Ethics of Social Cooperation

The Foundation for Economic Education, Inc.
30 South Broadway
Irvington-on-Hudson, NY 10533

Publisher's Cataloging in Publication
(Prepared by Quality Books, Inc.)

Hazlitt, Henry, 1894–
    [Foundations of morality]
    Rules for living : the ethics of social
cooperation : an abridgement of The foundations of
morality / by Henry Hazlitt ; edited by Bettina
Bien Greaves. — 1st ed.
    p. cm.
    Includes bibliographical references and index.
    LCCN: 98-73864
    ISBN: 1-57246-076-8

    1. Ethics.   I. Greaves, Bettina Bien. II.
Title.

BJ1012.H358   1999   170
                    QBI98-1761

Cover design by Beth R. Bowlby
Manufactured in the United States of America

Contents

Acknowledgments

In *The Foundations of Morality* Mr. Hazlitt acknowledged the permission he had received from publishers to quote from the several works cited. Some of the quotations in that book have been deleted from this abridgment. However, the Foundation for Economic Education would like once more to thank the publishers of the works from which quotations have been retained: Routledge & Kegan Paul, Ltd., of London, publisher of Philip H. Wicksteed's *The Common Sense of Political Economy;* The University of Chicago Press, publisher of F. A. Hayek's *The Constitution of Liberty;* and Yale University Press, publisher of Ludwig von Mises's *Human Action.*

Thanks should also go to the estate of Morris Raphael Cohen for having granted permission to quote from Cohen's *Faith of a Liberal.*

Maribel Montgomery of Albany, Oregon, deserves special credit for suggesting and supporting the publication of this abridgment of *The Foundations of Morality* and for having carefully selected the chapters to be included.

BBG

Introduction

"Everything that serves to preserve the social order is moral; everything that is detrimental to it is immoral."

—LUDWIG VON MISES, *Liberalism*

This book is an abridgment of Henry Hazlitt's *The Foundations of Morality* (first edition, 1964; second edition, 1972). In his 1963 Preface to that book, Mr. Hazlitt wrote that he believed progress in ethics was no less possible than in other branches of knowledge and thought. He hoped to contribute something to our understanding of ethics and morality by bringing together the teachings of other disciplines, especially economics and jurisprudence.

Hazlitt was an economic journalist of note, the author of the best-selling *Economics in One Lesson* and business columnist for *Newsweek*. Countless editorials and book reviews by him had been published in the *New York Times* and other newspapers. His familiarity with economics led him to reject the thesis of many moral philosophers that the interests of the individual and the interests of society were in opposition. His studies in the field of human action had convinced him that "modern economics had worked out answers to the problems of individual and social value of which most contemporary moral philosophers still seem quite unaware." Thus, he believed that ethical theory had a great deal to learn from modern economics. Ethical theory could also learn from jurisprudence, especially respecting "the immense importance of acting in strict accordance with established general rules."

"When the rightly understood interests of the individual are considered in the long run," Hazlitt wrote, "they are found to be in harmony with and to coincide (almost if not quite to the point of

v

identity) with the long-run interest of society. And to recognize this," Hazlitt wrote, "leads us to recognize conduciveness to social cooperation as the great criterion of the rightness of action, because voluntary social cooperation is the great means for the attainment not only of our collective but of nearly all our individual ends." This reasoning led Hazlitt to agree with his close friend and mentor, the Austrian economist Ludwig von Mises, quoted above, that the criterion for making moral judgments was simply whether or not it fostered or hindered social cooperation. To Hazlitt, however, the ethical implications of this position called for further elaboration than Mises gave them in his many economic writings. Hence *The Foundations of Morality.*

This abridgment attempts to include the most important themes presented by Hazlitt in *The Foundations of Morality.* It is not intended to supersede the longer work. It is offered to those who are interested in the conclusions derived from exploring the age-old philosophical controversy over morality. Of course readers who wish to pursue these issues further may refer to the longer work.

—BETTINA BIEN GREAVES

Foreword

Any sensible policy position presupposes understanding the reality that the natural and social sciences investigate. It also presupposes value judgments—notions of good and bad, desirable and undesirable, right and wrong. Ethics thus enters not only into private lives but also into public policy. But what is the grounding of ethics?

For many decades, utilitarian ethics has undeservedly had a bad press, not least in libertarian circles. It draws scorn as the mindset of crass, grasping, unprincipled people. It supposedly invites government hyperactivity aimed at maximizing some misconceived aggregate welfare. The critics would instead ground ethics and policy in noble and intuitively obvious principles such as unswerving respect for human dignity and natural human rights.

In this hostile intellectual atmosphere, Henry Hazlitt forthrightly and courageously avows a utilitarian ethics (although he did seek a more attractive label, perhaps cooperatism). Two classical-liberal think tanks, earlier the Institute for Humane Studies and now FEE, also deserve admiration for keeping his book in print. Hazlitt does not scorn human dignity and rights—of course not. But precisely because they are important, those values deserve a solider grounding than mere intuitions reported in noble-sounding language. The inviolability of rights rests, he says, "not . . . on some mystical yet self-evident 'law of nature' . . . [but] ultimately (though it will shock many to hear this) on utilitarian considerations." [p. 112 in this abridgment] Utilitarian philosophers can give reasons, grounded in reality, for respecting cherished values and the standard precepts of morality.

The bare facts of objective reality cannot by themselves provide this grounding. Some fundamental value judgment (or conceivably more than one) is also necessary, a judgment so ultimate that it lies beyond any series of reasons one might offer. Examples of relatively *specific* value judgments, in contrast, are the standard condemnations of murder, lying, cheating, and stealing. For them, one can give reasons that adduce the realities of human affairs, as well as some further and fundamental intuition. Only sloppy ethical theorizing appeals to a variety of specific intuitions instead of to one broad and fundamental value judgment. In a chapter omitted from this new edition, Hazlitt recommends applying Occam's razor to the promiscuous multiplication of alleged intuitions.

The one fundamental intuition of utilitarianism is approval of human flourishing, of people's success in making good lives for themselves, and disapproval of the opposite conditions. To use a single word for each, though each word requires much unpacking, utilitarianism welcomes happiness and regrets misery. This is a tame value judgment, to be sure; but combined with positive knowledge of the physical world and human affairs, it goes a long way in ethics. What fundamental value judgment or criterion could be more plausible?

Henry Hazlitt's great insight, following writers like David Hume and Ludwig von Mises, is that direct appeal to the criterion of happiness over misery is seldom necessary. A surrogate criterion is more tractable. Mises and Hazlitt call it "social cooperation." It means a well-functioning society, one in which people live together peaceably to their mutual advantage, all reaping gains from specialization and trade, trade not only in the narrow business sense but also in the informal interactions and mutual accommodations and courtesies of everyday life. Actions, institutions, rules, principles, customs, ideals, dispositions, and character traits count as good or bad according as they support or undercut such a society, which is prerequisite to the happiness of its members. Economics and the other social and natural sciences have much to say about what does support or undercut social cooperation.

Hazlitt gives powerful reasons for repudiating the brand of utilitarianism ("act-utilitarianism") that calls for whatever action seems most likely, on each particular occasion, to contribute most to the sum total of happiness. Although that brand has now sunk almost to the status of a mere straw man, it remains the favorite target of superficial critics of utilitarianism. Hazlitt advocates "rules-utilitarianism" instead, which, following John Gray's reading of John Stuart Mill, might better be named "indirect utilitarianism." Hazlitt calls for adherence, almost without exception, to ethical principles that do satisfy the utilitarian criterion.

Hazlitt also argues that the interests of the individual are not fundamentally in opposition to those of "society." A person's rightly conceived or long-run self-interest coincides with what serves social cooperation. (This reconciliation holds in a long-run or probabilistic sense, as the Austrian philosopher Moritz Schlick and others have explained; for life offers no absolute guarantees.)

Of all of Hazlitt's books on various topics and of all books on ethics that I have read, *The Foundations of Morality* is my favorite by far. Hazlitt himself, in a 1977 interview, called it his own favorite among the fifteen books he had then written. Yet—let us face the fact—it has so far made only a small splash among academic philosophers and economists. Why? One reason, I suppose, is that Hazlitt lacked the standard academic credentials. He was a profoundly educated man, but mostly self-educated. Holding no professorship, he could form no school of students and disciples. The book itself, with its many long direct quotations from other writers, may have repelled potential readers who merely flipped through it. But Hazlitt chose his quotations remarkably well, and they do help carry his own argument forward.

This new edition omits many of those quotations. It is not a condensation of the *Reader's Digest* sort. That sort, as I understand it, tries to squeeze out superfluous words by rewriting even individual sentences and paragraphs. Hazlitt's excellent writing style leaves little scope for such tightening. Instead, large chunks of text have been omitted, including whole paragraphs, quotations, and especially whole chapters—18 out of 33. I was sorry to see the sacrifice of chapters on "Satisfaction and Happiness," "Prudence and Benevolence," "Egoism, Altruism, Mutualism," "Duty for Duty's Sake," "The Law of Nature," and "Justice."

On the other hand, this shortened edition will attract new readers and new adherents to the intelligent utilitarianism that provides (in my view) the soundest philosophical basis for the humane society that is the ideal of classical liberals. Many of these new readers, we may hope, will go on to study the uncut version of *The Foundations of Morality,* which FEE is also keeping in print.

—LELAND B. YEAGER

* *Ludwig von Mises Distinguished Professor of Economics Emeritus at Auburn University, Alabama*
* *Paul Goodlow McIntire Professor of Economics Emeritus at the University of Virginia*

March 1998

CHAPTER 1

The Mystery of Morals

Each of us has grown up in a world in which moral judgments already exist. These judgments are passed every day by everyone on the conduct of everyone else. Each of us not only finds himself approving or disapproving how other people act, but approving or disapproving certain actions, and even certain *rules* or *principles* of action, wholly apart from his feelings about those who perform or follow them. So deep does this go that most of us even apply these judgments to our own conduct, and approve or disapprove of our own conduct insofar as we judge it to have conformed to the principles or standards by which we judge others. When we have failed, in our own judgment, to live up to the moral code which we habitually apply to others, we feel "guilty"; our "conscience" bothers us.

Our personal moral standards may not be precisely the same in all respects as those of our friends or neighbors or countrymen, but they are remarkably similar. We find greater differences when we compare "national" standards with those of other countries, and perhaps still greater differences when we compare them with the moral standards of people in the distant past. But in spite of these greater differences, we seem to find, for the most part, a persistent core of similarity, and persistent judgments which condemn such traits as cruelty, cowardice, and treachery, or such actions as lying, theft, or murder.

None of us can remember when we first began to pass judgments of moral approval or disapproval. From infancy we found such judgments being passed upon us by our parents—"good" baby, "bad" baby—and from infancy we passed such judgments indiscriminately on persons, animals, and things—"good" playmate or "bad" play-mate, "good" dog or "bad" dog, and even "bad" doorknob if we

1

bumped our head against it. Only gradually did we begin to distinguish approval or disapproval on moral grounds from approval or disapproval on other grounds.

Implicit moral codes probably existed for centuries before they were made explicit—as in the Decalogue, or the sacred law of Manu, or the code of Hammurabi. And it was long after they had first been made explicit, in speech or writing, in proverbs or commands or laws, that men began to speculate about them, and began consciously to search for a common explanation or rationale.

And then they were faced with a great mystery. How had such a code of morals come into being? Why did it consist of a certain set of commands and not others? Why did it forbid certain actions? Why only *these* actions? Why did it enjoin or command other actions? And how did men *know* that certain actions were "right" and others "wrong"?

The first theory was that certain actions were "right" and others "wrong" because God (or the gods) had so decreed. Certain actions were pleasing to God (or the gods) and certain others displeasing. Certain actions would be rewarded by God, here or hereafter, and certain other actions would be punished by God, here or hereafter.

This theory, or faith, held the field for centuries. It is still, probably, the dominant popular theory or faith. But among philosophers, even among the early Christian philosophers, it met with two difficulties. The first was this: Was this moral code, then, merely arbitrary? Were certain actions right and others wrong merely because God had so willed? Or was not the causation, rather, the other way round? God's divine nature could not will what was evil, but only what was good. He could not decree what was wrong, but only what was right. But this argument implied that Good and Evil, Right and Wrong, were independent of, and pre-existent to, God's will.

There was a second difficulty. Even if Good and Evil, Right and Wrong, were determined by God's will, how were we mortals to know God's will? The question was answered simply enough, perhaps, for the ancient Jews: God himself dictated the Ten Commandments—and hundreds of other laws and judgments—to Moses on Mount Sinai. God, in fact, wrote the Ten Commandments with his own finger on tablets of stone.

Yet numerous as the commandments and judgments were, they did not clearly distinguish in importance and degree of sinfulness between committing murder and working on the Sabbath day. They have not been and cannot consistently be a guide for Christians. Christians ignore the dietary laws prescribed by the God of Moses. The God of Moses commanded "Eye for eye, tooth for tooth, hand for hand, foot for foot, burning for burning, wound for wound, stripe for stripe" (Exodus 21:24,25). But Jesus commanded: "Whosoever shall smite thee on thy right cheek, turn to him the other also" (Matthew 5:39); "Love your enemies, bless them that curse you, do good to them that hate you" (Matthew 5:44); "A new commandment I give unto you, that ye love one another" (John 13:34).

The problem then remains: How can we, how do we, tell right from wrong? Another answer, still offered by many ethical writers, is that we do so by a special "moral sense" or by direct "intuition." The difficulty here is not only that one man's moral sense or intuition gives different answers than another's, but that a man's moral sense or intuition often fails to provide a clear answer even when he consults it.

A third answer is that our moral code is a product of gradual social evolution, like language, or manners, or the common law, and that, like them, it has grown and evolved to meet the need for peace and order and social cooperation.

A fourth answer is that of simple ethical skepticism or nihilism which affects to regard all moral rules or judgments as the product of baseless superstition. But this nihilism is never consistent and seldom sincere. If one who professed it were knocked down, brutally beaten, and robbed, he would feel something remarkably similar to moral indignation, and he would express his feeling in words very hard to distinguish from those of moral disapproval.

A less violent way to convert the moral nihilist, however, would be simply to ask him to imagine a society in which no moral code existed, or in which it were the exact opposite of the codes we customarily find. We might ask him to imagine how long a society (or the individuals in it) could prosper or even continue to exist in which ill manners, promise-breaking, ingratitude, disloyalty, treachery, violence, and chaos were the rule, and were as highly regarded as, or even more highly regarded than, their opposites—good manners, promise-keeping, truth-telling, honesty, fairness, loyalty, consideration for others, peace and order, and social cooperation.

But false theories of ethics, and the number of possible fallacies in ethics, are almost infinite. We can deal only with a few of the major fallacies that have been maintained historically or that are still widely held. It would be unprofitable and uneconomic to explain in detail why each false theory is wrong or inadequate, unless we first tried to find the true foundations of morality and a reasonably satisfactory outline of a system of ethics. If we once find the right answer, it will be much easier to see and to explain why other answers are wrong or, at best, half-truths. Our analysis of errors will then be at once clearer and more economical. And we shall use such analysis of errors to sharpen our positive theory and make it more precise.

Now there are two main methods which we might use to formulate a theory of ethics. The first might be what we may call, for identification rather than accuracy, the *inductive* or *a posteriori* method. This would consist in examining what our moral judgments of various acts or characteristics actually are, and then trying to see whether they form a consistent whole, and on what common principle or criterion, if any, they rest. The second would be the *a priori* or *deductive* method. This would consist in disregarding existing moral judgments; in asking ourselves whether a moral code would serve any purpose, and if so, what that purpose would be; and then, having framed the purpose, asking ourselves what principle, criterion, or code would accomplish that purpose. In other words, we would try to *invent* a system of morality, and then test existing moral judgments by the criterion at which we had deductively arrived.

The second was essentially the method of Jeremy Bentham, the first the method of more cautious thinkers. The second, by itself, would be rash and arrogant; the first, by itself, might prove to be too timid. But as practically all fruitful thinking consists of a judicious mixture—the "inductive-deductive" method —so we shall find ourselves using now one method and now another.

Let us begin by looking for the Ultimate Moral Criterion.

CHAPTER 2

The Moral Criterion

Speculative thought comes late in the history of mankind. Men act before they philosophize about their actions. They learned to talk, and developed language, ages before they developed any interest in grammar or linguistics. They worked and saved, planted crops, fashioned tools, built homes, owned, bartered, bought and sold, and developed money, long before they formulated any explicit theories of economics. They developed forms of government and law, and even judges and courts, before they formulated theories of politics or jurisprudence. And they acted implicitly in accordance with a code of morals, rewarded or punished, approved or disapproved of the actions of their fellows in adhering to or violating that code of morals, long before it even occurred to them to inquire into the rationale of what they were doing.

It would seem at first glance both natural and logical, therefore, to begin the study of ethics with an inquiry into the history or evolution of ethical practice and judgments. Certainly we should engage in such an inquiry at some time in the course of our study. Yet ethics is perhaps the one discipline where it seems more profitable to begin at the other end. For ethics is a "normative" science. It is not a science of *de*scription, but of *pre*scription. It is not a science of what is or was, but of what *ought* to be.

True, it would have no claim to scientific validity, or even any claim to be a useful field of inquiry, unless it were based in some convincing way on what was or what is. But here we have stepped into the very center of an age-old controversy. Many ethical writers have contended during the last two centuries that "no accumulation of observed sequences, no experience of what *is,* no predictions of what *will be,* can possibly prove what *ought to be.*"[1] And others have even gone on to assert that there is no way of getting from an *is* to an *ought.*

If the latter statement were true, there would be no possibility of framing a rational theory of ethics. Unless our *oughts* are to be purely arbitrary, purely dogmatic, they must somehow grow out of what *is.*

Now the connection between what is and what ought to be is always a *desire* of some kind. We recognize this in our daily decisions. When we are trying to decide on a course of action, and are asking advice, we are told, for example: "If you desire to become a doctor, you must go to medical school. If you desire to get ahead, you must be diligent in your business. If you don't want to get fat, you must watch your diet. If you want to avoid lung cancer, you must cut down on cigarettes," etc. The generalized form of such advice may be reduced to this: *If* you desire to attain a certain *end,* you *ought* to use a certain means, because this is the means most likely to achieve it. The *is* is the desire; the *ought* is the means of gratifying it.

So far, so good. But how far does this get us toward a theory of ethics? For if a man does not desire an end, there seems no way of convincing him that he ought to pursue the means to that end. If a man prefers the certainty of getting fat, or the risk of a heart attack, to curbing his appetite or giving up his favorite delicacies; if he prefers the risks of lung cancer to giving up smoking, any *ought* based on the assumption of a contrary preference loses its force.

A story so old that it is told as an old one even by Bentham[2] is that of the oculist and the sot: A countryman who had hurt his eyes by drinking went to a celebrated oculist for advice. He found him at table, with a glass of wine before him. "You must leave off drinking," said the oculist. "How so?" says the countryman. *"You* don't, and yet methinks your own eyes are none of the best."—"That's very true, friend," replied the oculist: "but you are to know, I love my bottle better than my eyes."

How, then, do we move from any basis of desire to any theory of ethics?

We find the solution when we take a longer and broader view. All our desires may be generalized as desires to substitute a more satisfactory state of affairs for a less satisfactory state. It is true that an individual, under the immediate influence of impulse or passion, of a moment of anger or rage, malice, vindictiveness, or the desire for revenge, or gluttony, or an overwhelming craving for a release of sexual tension, or for a smoke or a drink or a drug, may in the long run only reduce a more satisfactory state to a less satisfactory state, may make himself less happy rather than more happy. But this less satisfactory state was not his real conscious intention even at the moment of acting. He realizes, in retrospect, that his action was folly; he did not improve his condition, but made it worse; he did not act in accordance with his long-run interests, but against them. He is always willing to recognize, in his calmer moments, that he should choose the action that best promotes his own interests and maximizes his own happiness (or minimizes his own unhappiness) *in the long run*. Wise and disciplined men refuse to indulge in immediate pleasures when the indulgence seems only too likely to lead in the long run to an overbalance of misery or pain.

To repeat and to sum up: It is not true that "no amount of *is* can make an *ought*." The *ought* rests, in fact, and must rest, either upon an *is* or upon a *will be*. The sequence is simple: Every man, in his cool and rational moments, seeks his own long-run happiness. This is a *fact;* this is an *is*. Mankind has found, over the centuries, that certain rules of action best tend to promote the long-run happiness of both the individual and society. These rules of action have come to be called *moral* rules. Therefore, assuming that one seeks one's long-run happiness, these are the rules one *ought* to follow.

Certainly this is the whole basis of what is called *prudential* ethics. In fact, wisdom, or the art of living wisely, is perhaps only another name for prudential ethics.

Prudential ethics constitutes a very large part of all ethics. But the whole of ethics rests upon the same foundation. For men find that they best promote their own interests in the long run not merely by refraining from injury to their fellows, but by cooperating with them. Social cooperation is the foremost means by which the majority of us attain most of our ends. It is on the implicit if not the explicit recognition of this that our codes of morals, our rules of conduct, are ultimately based.

Social cooperation is, of course, itself a means. It is a means to the never completely attainable goal of maximizing the happiness and well-being of mankind. But the great difficulty of making the latter our direct goal is the lack of unanimity in the tastes, ends, and value judgments of individuals. An activity that gives one man pleasure may be a great bore to another. "One man's meat is another man's poison." But social cooperation is the great means by which we all help each other to attain our individual ends, and so to attain the ends of "society." Moreover, we do share a great number of basic ends in common; and social cooperation is the principal means of attaining these also.

In brief, the aim of each of us to satisfy his own desires, to achieve as far as possible his own highest happiness and well-being, is best forwarded by a common means, Social Cooperation, and cannot be achieved without that means.

Here, then, is the foundation on which we may build a rational system of ethics.

---

1. Hastings Rashdall, *The Theory of Good and Evil* (London: Oxford University Press, 1907), I, p. 53.

2. Jeremy Bentham, *An Introduction to the Principles of Morals and Legislation* (Oxford: Clarendon Press, 1823), p. 319n.

CHAPTER 3

Social Cooperation

1. Each and All

The ultimate goal of the conduct of each of us, as an individual, is to maximize his own happiness and well-being. Therefore the effort of each of us, as a member of society, is to persuade and induce *everybody else* to act so as to maximize the long-run happiness and well-being of society as a whole and even, if necessary, forcibly to prevent anybody from acting to reduce or destroy the happiness or well-being of society as a whole. For the happiness and well-being of each is promoted by the same conduct that promotes the happiness and well-being of all. Conversely, the happiness and well-being of all is promoted by the conduct that promotes the happiness and well-being of each. In the long run the aims of the individual and "society" (considering this as the name that each of us gives to all *other* individuals) coalesce, and tend to coincide.

We may state this conclusion in another form: The aim of each of us is to maximize his own satisfaction; and each of us recognizes that his satisfaction can best be maximized by cooperating with others and having others cooperate with him. Society itself, therefore, may be defined as nothing else but the combination of individuals for cooperative effort.[1] If we keep this in mind, there is no harm in saying that, as it is the aim of each of us to maximize his satisfactions, so it is the aim of "society" to maximize the satisfactions of each of its members, or, where this cannot be completely done, to try to reconcile and harmonize as many desires as possible, and to minimize the dissatisfactions or maximize the satisfactions of as many persons as possible in the long run.

Thus our goal envisions continuously both a present state of well-being and a future state of well-being, the maximization of both present satisfactions and future satisfactions.

But this statement of the ultimate goal carries us only a little way toward a system of ethics.

2. The Way to the Goal

It was an error of most of the older utilitarians, as of earlier moralists, to suppose that if they could once find and state the ultimate goal of conduct, the great *Summum Bonum,* their mission was completed. They were like medieval knights devoting all their efforts to the quest of the Holy Grail, and assuming that, if they once found it, their task would be done.

Yet even if we assume that we have found, or succeeded in stating, the "ultimate" goal of conduct, we have no more finished our task than if we had decided to go to the Holy Land. We must know the way to get there. We must know the means, and the means of obtaining the means.

By what means are we to achieve the goal of conduct? How are we to know what conduct is most likely to achieve this goal?

The great problem presented by ethics is that no two people find their happiness or satisfactions in precisely the same things. Each of us has his own peculiar set of desires, his own particular valuations, his own intermediate ends. Unanimity in value judgments does not exist, and probably never will.

This seems to present a dilemma, a logical dead end, from which the older ethical writers struggled for a way of escape. Many of them thought they had found it in the doctrine that ultimate goals and ethical rules were known by "intuition." When there was disagreement about these goals or rules, they tried to resolve it by consulting their own individual consciences, and taking their own private intuitions as the guide. This was not a good way out. Yet a way of escape from the dilemma was there.

This lies in *Social Cooperation.* For each of us, social cooperation is the great means of attaining nearly all our ends. For each of us social cooperation is of course not the ultimate end but a means. It has the great advantage that no unanimity with regard to value judgments is required to make it work.[2] But it is a means so central, so universal, so indispensable to the realization of practically all our other ends, that there is little harm in regarding it as an end-in-itself, and even in treating it as if it were *the* goal of ethics. In fact, precisely because none of us knows *exactly* what would give most satisfaction or happiness to others, the best test of our actions or rules of action is the extent to which they promote a social cooperation that best enables each of us to pursue *his own* ends.

Without social cooperation modern man could not achieve the barest fraction of the ends and satisfactions that he has achieved with it. The very subsistence of the immense majority of us depends upon it. We cannot treat subsistence as basely material and beneath our moral notice. As Ludwig von Mises reminds us: "Even the most sublime ends cannot be sought by people who have not first satisfied the wants of their animal body."[3] And as Philip Wicksteed has more concretely put it: "A man can be neither a saint, nor a lover, nor a poet, unless he has comparatively recently had something to eat."[4]

3. The Division of Labor

The great means of social cooperation is the division and combination of labor. The division of labor enormously increases the productivity of each of us and therefore the productivity of all of us. This has been recognized since the very beginning of economics as a science. Its recognition is, indeed, the foundation of modern economics. It is not mere coincidence that the statement of this truth occurs in the very first sentence of the first chapter of Adam Smith's great *Wealth of Nations,* published in 1776: "The greatest improvement in the productive powers of labor, and the greater part of the skill, dexterity, and judgment with which it is any where directed, or applied, seem to have been the effects of the division of labor."

Adam Smith goes on to take an example from "a very trifling manufacture; but one in which the division of labor has been very often taken notice of, the trade of the pin-maker." He points out that "a workman not educated to this business (which the division of labor has rendered a distinct trade), nor acquainted with the use of machinery employed in it (to the invention of which the same division of labor has probably given occasion), could scarce, perhaps, with the utmost industry, make one pin a day, and certainly could not make twenty." In the way in which the work is actually carried on (in 1776), he tells us: "One man draws out the wire, another straights it, a third cuts it, a fourth points it, a fifth grinds it at the top for receiving the head" and so on, so that "the important business of making a pin is, in this manner, divided into about eighteen distinct operations." He tells how he himself has seen "a small manufactory of this kind where ten men only were employed" yet "could make among them upwards of forty-eight thousand pins in a day. Each person, therefore, making a tenth part of forty-eight thousand pins, might be considered as making four thousand eight hundred pins in a day. But if they had all wrought separately and independently and without any of them having been educated to this peculiar business, they certainly could not each of them have made twenty, perhaps not one pin a day; that is, certainly, not the two hundred and fortieth, perhaps not the four thousand eight hundredth part of what they are at present capable of performing, in consequence of a proper division and combination of their different operations."

Smith then goes on to show, from further illustrations, how "the division of labor . . . so far as it can be introduced, occasions, in every art, a proportionable increase of the productive powers of labor"; and how "the separation of different trades and employments from one another seems to have taken place in consequences of this advantage."

This great increase in productivity he attributes to "three different circumstances; first, to the increase of dexterity in every particular workman; secondly, to the saving of the time which is commonly lost in passing from one species of work to another; and lastly, to the invention of a great number of machines which facilitate and abridge labor, and enable one man to do the work of many." These three "circumstances" are then explained in detail.

"It is the great multiplication of the productions of all the different arts, in consequence of the division of labor," Smith concludes, "which occasions, in a well-governed society, that universal opulence which extends itself to the lowest ranks of the people."

But this brings him to a further question, which he proceeds to take up in his second chapter. "This division of labor, from which so many advantages are derived, is not originally the effect of any human wisdom, which foresees and intends that general opulence to which it gives occasion. It is the necessary, though very slow and gradual, consequence of a certain propensity in human nature which has in view no such extensive utility; the propensity to truck, barter, and exchange one thing for another."

In resting the origin of the division of labor on an unexplained "propensity to truck, barter, and exchange," as he sometimes seems to do in his succeeding argument, Adam Smith was wrong. Social cooperation and the division of labor rest upon a recognition (though often implicit rather than explicit) on the part of the individual that this promotes his own self-interest— that work performed under the division of labor is more productive than isolated work. And in fact, Adam Smith's own subsequent argument in Chapter II clearly recognizes this:

> In civilized society [the individual] stands at all times in need of the cooperation and assistance of great multitudes. . . . Man has almost constant occasion for the help of his brethren, and it is in vain for him to expect it from their benevolence only. He will be more likely to prevail if he can interest their self-love in his favor, and show them that it is

for their own advantage to do for him what he requires of them. Whoever offers to another a bargain of any kind, proposes to do this: Give me that which I want, and you shall have this which you want, is the meaning of every such offer; and it is in this manner that we obtain from one another the far greater part of those good offices which we stand in need of. It is not from the benevolence of the butcher, the brewer, or the baker, that we expect our dinner, but from their regard to their own interest. We address ourselves, not to their humanity but to their self-love, and never talk to them of our own necessities but of their advantages.

"Nobody but a beggar," Smith points out in extending the argument, "chooses to depend chiefly upon the benevolence of his fellow citizens," and "even a beggar does not depend upon it entirely," for "with the money which one man gives him he purchases food," etc.

"As it is by treaty, by barter, and by purchase," Adam Smith continues, "that we obtain from one another the greater part of those mutual good offices which we stand in need of, so it is this same trucking disposition which originally gives occasion to the division of labor. In a tribe of hunters or shepherds a particular person makes bows and arrows, for example, with more readiness and dexterity than any other. He frequently exchanges them for cattle or for venison with his companions; and he finds at last that he can in this manner get more cattle and venison, than if he himself went to the field to catch them. From a regard to his own interest, therefore, the making of bows and arrows grows to be his chief business, and he becomes a sort of armourer." And Smith explains how in turn other specialists develop.

In brief, each of us, in pursuing his self-interest, finds that he can do it most effectively through social cooperation. The belief that there is a basic conflict between the interests of the individual and the interests of society is untenable. Society is only another name for the combination of individuals for purposeful cooperation.

4. The Basis of Economic Life

Let us look a little more closely at the motivational basis of this great system of social cooperation through exchange of goods or services. I have just used the phrase "self-interest," following Adam Smith's example when he speaks of the butcher's and the baker's "own interests," "self-love," and "advantage." But we should be careful not to assume that people enter into these economic relations with each other simply because each seeks only his "selfish" or "egoistic" advantage. Let us see how an acute economist restates the essence of this economic relation.

The economic life, writes Philip Wicksteed, "consists of all that complex of relations into which we enter with other people, and lend ourselves or our resources to the furtherance of their purposes as an indirect means of furthering our own."[5] "By direct and indirect processes of exchange, by the social alchemy of which money is the symbol, the things I have and the things I can [do] are transmuted into the things I want and the things I would."[6] People cooperate with me in the economic relation "not primarily, or not solely, because they are interested in my purposes, but because they have certain purposes of their own; and just as I find that I can only secure the accomplishment of my purposes by securing their cooperation, so they find that they can only accomplish theirs by securing the cooperation of yet others, and they find that I am in a position, directly or indirectly, to place this cooperation at their disposal. A vast range, therefore, of our relations with others enters into a system of mutual adjustment by which we further each other's purposes simply as an indirect way of furthering our own."[7]

So far the reader may not have detected any substantial difference between Wicksteed's statement and Adam Smith's. Yet there is a very important one. I enter into an economic or business relation with you, for the exchange of goods or services for money, primarily to further *my* purposes, not yours, and you enter into it, on your side, primarily to further *your* purposes, not mine. But this does not mean that either of our purposes is necessarily selfish or self-centered. I may be hiring your services as a printer to publish a tract at my own expense pleading for more kindness to animals. A mother buying groceries in the market will go where she can get the best quality or the lowest price, and not to help any particular grocer; yet in buying her groceries she may have the needs and tastes of her husband or children in mind more than her own needs or tastes. "When Paul of Tarsus abode with Aquila and Priscilla in Corinth and wrought with them at his craft of tent-making we shall hardly say that he was inspired by egoistic motives. . . . The economic relation, then, or business nexus, is necessary alike for carrying on the life of the peasant and the prince, of the saint and the sinner, of the apostle and the shepherd, of the most altruistic and the most egoistic of men."[8]

The reader may have begun to wonder at this point whether this is a book on ethics or on economics. But I have emphasized this economic cooperation because it occupies so enormous a part of our daily life. It plays, in fact, a far larger role in our daily life than most of us are consciously aware of. The relationship of employer and employee (notwithstanding the misconceptions and propaganda of the Marxist socialists and the unions) is essentially a cooperative relationship. Each needs the other to accomplish his own purposes. The success of the employer depends upon the industriousness, skill, and loyalty of his employees; the jobs and incomes of the employees depend upon the success of the employer. Even economic competition, so commonly regarded by socialists and reformers as a form of economic warfare,[9] is part of a great system of social cooperation, which promotes continual invention and improvement of products, continual reduction of costs and prices, continual widening of the range of choice and continual increase of the welfare of consumers. The competition for workers constantly raises wages, as the competition for jobs improves performance and efficiency. True, competitors do not cooperate *directly* with each other; but each, in competing for the patronage of third parties, seeks to offer more advantages to those third parties than his rival can, and in so doing each forwards the whole system of social cooperation. Economic competition is simply the striving of individuals to attain the most favorable position in the system of social cooperation. As such, it must exist in any conceivable mode of social organization.[10]

The realm of economic cooperation, as I have said, occupies a far larger part of our daily life than most of us are commonly aware of, or even willing to admit. Marriage and the family are, among other things, a form not only of biological but of economical cooperation. In primitive societies the man hunted and fished while the woman prepared the food. In modern society the husband is still responsible for the physical protection and the food supply of his wife and children. Each member of the family gains by this cooperation, and it is largely on recognition of this mutual economic gain, and not merely of the joys of love and companionship, that the foundations of the institution of marriage are so solidly built.

But though the advantages of social cooperation are to an enormous extent economic, they are not solely economic. Through social cooperation we promote all the values, direct and indirect, material and spiritual, cultural and aesthetic, of modern civilization.

Some readers will see a similarity, and others may suspect an identity, between the ideal of Social Cooperation and Kropotkin's ideal of "Mutual Aid."[11] A similarity there surely is. But Social Cooperation seems to me not only a much more appropriate *phrase* than Mutual Aid, but a much more appropriate and precise *concept.* Typical instances of cooperation occur when two men row a boat or paddle a canoe from opposite sides, when four men move a piano or a crate by lifting opposite corners, when a carpenter hires a helper, when an orchestra plays a symphony. We would not hesitate to say that any of these were cooperative undertakings or acts of cooperation, but we should be surprised to find all of them called examples of "mutual aid." For "aid" carries the implication of *gratuitous* help—the rich aiding the poor, the strong aiding the weak, the superior, out of compassion, aiding the inferior. It also seems to carry the implication of *haphazard* and *sporadic* rather than of *systematic* and *continuous* cooperation. The phrase Social Cooperation, on the other hand, seems to cover not only everything that the phrase Mutual Aid implies but the very purpose and basis of life in society.[12]

---

1. *Cf.* Ludwig von Mises, *Human Action* (New Haven: Yale University Press, 1949), p. 143.

2. *Cf.* Ludwig von Mises, *Theory and History* (New Haven: Yale University Press, 1957), pp. 55–61.

3. *Ibid.,* p. 57.

4. Philip H. Wicksteed, *The Common Sense of Political Economy* (London: Routledge & Kegan Paul, 1910), p. 154.

5. *Ibid.,* p. 158.

6. *Ibid.,* p. 166.

7. *Loc. cit.*

8. *Ibid.,* pp. 170–171.

9. As used, for instance, by Bertrand Russell, *passim.*

10. *Cf.* Ludwig von Mises, *Human Action,* pp. 273ff.

11. Prince Kropotkin, *Ethics: Origin and Development* (New York: The Dial Press, 1924), pp. 30–31 and *passim.* Also, *Mutual Aid, A Factor of Evolution* (London: Heineman, 1915). Kropotkin's ethical ideas were based in large part on biological theories. As against Nietzsche (and in part Herbert Spencer) he contended that not the "struggle for existence" but Mutual Aid is "the predominant fact of nature," the prevailing practice within the species, and "the chief factor of progressive evolution."

12. The phrase "social cooperation," in this chapter and throughout the book, is of course to be interpreted only in its most comprehensive meaning. It is not intended to refer to "cooperation" between individuals or groups *against* other individuals or groups—as when we speak of cooperation with the Nazis, or the Communists, or the enemy. Nor is it intended to refer to that kind of compulsory

"cooperation" that superiors sometimes insist on from subordinates—unless this is compatible with a comprehensive cooperation with the aims of society as a whole. Nor is it, for the same reason, intended to apply to cooperation with a mere temporary or local majority, when this is incompatible with a broader cooperation for the achievement of human aims.

CHAPTER 4

Long Run *vs.* Short Run

1. The Voluptuary's Fallacy

There is no irreconcilable conflict between the interests of the individual and those of society. If there were, society could not exist. Society is the great means through which individuals pursue and fulfill their ends. For society is but another name for the combination of individuals for cooperation. It is the means through which each of us furthers the purposes of others as an indirect means of furthering his own. And this cooperation is in the overwhelming main *voluntary*. It is only collectivists who assume that the interests of the individual and of society (or the State) are fundamentally opposed, and that the individual can only be led to cooperate in society by Draconian compulsions.

The real distinction we need to make for ethical clarity is not that between the individual and society, or even between "egoism" and "altruism," but between interests in the short run and those in the long run. This distinction is made constantly in modern economics.[1] It is in large part the basis for the condemnation by economists of such policies as tariffs, subsidies, price-fixing, rent control, crop supports, featherbedding, deficit-financing, and inflation. Those who say mockingly that "in the long run we are all dead"[2] are just as irresponsible as the French aristocrats whose reputed motto was *Après nous le déluge*.

The distinction between short-run interests and long-run interests has always been implicit in common sense ethical judgments, particularly as concerns prudential ethics. But it has seldom received explicit recognition, and more seldom still in those words.[3] The classical moralist who came nearest to stating it systematically is Jeremy Bentham. He does this, not in the form of comparing short-run interests with long-run interests, or short-run consequences of actions with long-run consequences, but in the form of comparing greater or smaller amounts of pleasure or happiness. Thus in his effort to judge actions by comparing the quantities or "values" of the pleasures they yield or lead to, he measures these quantities by "duration" (among seven standards) as well as by "intensity."[4] And in his *Deontology* a typical statement is: "Is not temperance a virtue? Aye, assuredly is it. But wherefore? Because by restraining enjoyment for a time, it afterwards elevates it to that very pitch which leaves, on the whole, the last addition to the stock of happiness."[5]

The common sense reasons for temperance and other prudential virtues are frequently misunderstood or derided by ethical skeptics:

Let us have wine and women, mirth and laughter,
Sermons and soda-water the day after.

So sang Byron. The implication is that the "sermons and soda-water," are a short and cheap price to pay for the fun. Samuel Butler, also, cynically generalized the distinction between morality and immorality as depending merely on the order of precedence between pleasure and pain: "Morality turns on whether the pleasure precedes or follows the pain. Thus it is immoral to get drunk because the headache comes after the drinking, but if the headache came first, and the drunkenness afterwards, it would be moral to get drunk."[6]

When we talk seriously, it is of course not at all a question whether the pain or the pleasure comes first, but which exceeds the other in the long run. The confusions that result from failure to understand this principle lead not only, on the one hand, to the sophisms of the ethical skeptics but, on the other, to the fallacies of anti-utilitarian writers and of ascetics. When the anti-utilitarians attack not merely the pleasure-pain calculus of the Benthamites but the Greatest Happiness Principle, or the maximization of satisfactions, it will be found that they are almost invariably assuming, tacitly or expressly, that the utilitarian standards take only immediate or short-run consequences into consideration. Their criticism is valid only as applied to crude forms of hedonistic and utilitarian theories.

2. The Ascetic's Fallacy

The confusion in another form leads to the opposite result—to the theories and standards of asceticism. The utilitarian standard, consistently applied, merely asks whether an action (or more properly a rule of action) will tend to lead to a surplus of happiness and well-being, or a surplus of unhappiness and ill-being, for all those whom it affects, in the long run. One of Bentham's great merits was that he attempted to apply the standard thoroughly and consistently. Though he was not wholly successful, because there were several important tools of analysis that he lacked, what is remarkable is the degree of his success, and the steadiness with which he kept this standard in mind.

In the interests of the individual's long-run well-being, it is necessary for him to make certain short-run sacrifices, or apparent sacrifices. He must put certain immediate restraints on his impulses in order to prevent later regrets. He must accept a certain deprivation today, either in order to reap a greater compensation in the future or to prevent an even greater deprivation in the future.

But ascetics, by a confused association, conclude that the restraint, deprivation, sacrifice, or pain that must sometimes be undergone in the present for the sake of the future, is something virtuous and praiseworthy for its own sake. Asceticism was caustically defined by Bentham as "that principle, which, like the principle of utility, approves or disapproves of any action, according to the tendency which it appears to have to augment or diminish the happiness of the party whose interest is in question; but in an inverse manner: approving of actions in as far as they tend to diminish his happiness; disapproving of them in as far as they tend to augment it."[7] And he continued: "It is evident that any one who reprobates any the least particle of pleasure, as such, from whatever source derived, is *pro tanto* a partizan of the principle of asceticism."[8]

A more favorable judgment of asceticism is possible if we give it another definition. As Bentham himself explained, it comes etymologically from a Greek word meaning *exercise.* Bentham then went on to declare that: "The practices by which Monks sought to distinguish themselves from other men were called their Exercises. These exercises consisted in so many contrivances they had for tormenting themselves."[9]

However if, rejecting this definition, we think of asceticism as a form of *athleticism,* analogous to the discipline that athletes or soldiers undergo to harden themselves against possible adversity, or against probable trials of strength, courage, fortitude, effort, and endurance in the future, or even as a process of restraint to sharpen "the keen edge of seldom pleasure," then it is something that serves a utilitarian and even a hedonistic purpose.

Confusion of thought will continue as long as we use the same word, *asceticism,* in both of these senses. We can avoid ambiguity only by assigning separate names to each meaning.

I am going to reject the semantic temptation to take advantage of the traditional moral prestige of the ascetic ideal by using *asceticism* only in the "good" sense of a far-sighted discipline or restraint undertaken to maximize one's happiness in the long run. If I did this, I would then be obliged to use exclusively some other word, such as *flagellantism,* for the "bad" sense of mortification or self-torment. No one can presume to set himself up as a dictator of verbal usage. I can only say, therefore, that in view of traditional usage I think it would be most honest and least confusing to confine the word *asceticism* to the anti-utilitarian, anti-hedonist, anti-eudae-monist* meaning of self-denial and self-torment for their own sakes, and to reserve another word, say *self-discipline,* or even to coin a word, like *disciplinism*[10] for the doctrine which believes in abstinence and restraint, not for their own sakes, but only in so far as they serve as means for increasing happiness in the long run.

The distinction between the consideration of short-run and long-run consequences is so basic, and applies so widely, that one might be excused for trying to make it, by itself, the whole foundation for a system of ethics, and to say, quite simply, that morality is essentially, not the subordination of the "individual" to "society" but the subordination of immediate objectives to long-term ones. Certainly the Long-Run Principle is a necessary if not a sufficient foundation for morality. Bentham did not have the concept (which has been made explicit mainly by modern economics) in just these words, but he came close to it in his constant insistence on the necessity of considering the future as well as the present consequences of any course of conduct, and in his attempt to measure and compare "quantities" of pleasure not merely in terms of "intensity" but of "duration." Many efforts have been made to define the difference between *pleasure* and *happiness.* One of them is surely that between a momentary gratification and a permanent or at least prolonged gratification, between the short run and the long run.

3. On Undervaluing the Future

Perhaps this is an appropriate point to warn the reader against some possible misinterpretations of the Long-Run Principle. When we are asked to take into consideration the probable consequences of a given act or rule of action in the long run, this does not mean that we must disregard, or even that we are justified in disregarding, its probable consequences in the short run. What we are really being

*Ed. note, Anti-pleasure-seeking.

asked to consider is the *total net* consequences of a given act or rule of action. We are justified in considering the pleasure of tonight's drinking against the pain of tomorrow's headache, the pleasure of tonight's eating against the pain of tomorrow's indigestion or unwelcome increase in weight, the pleasure of this summer's vacation in Europe against this fall's precarious bank balance. We should not be misled by the term "long run" into supposing that pleasure, satisfaction, or happiness is to be valued only, in accordance with its duration: its "intensity," "certainty," "propinquity," "fecundity," "purity," and "extent" also count. In this insight Bentham was correct. In the rare cases of conflict, it is the rule of action that promises to yield the *most* satisfaction, rather than merely the *longest* satisfaction, or merely the greatest *future* satisfaction, that we should choose. We need not value probable future satisfaction *above* present satisfaction. It is only because our human nature is too prone to yield to present impulse and forget the future cost that it is necessary to make a special effort to keep this future cost before the mind at the moment of temptation. If the immediate pleasure does indeed outweigh the probable future cost, then refusal to indulge oneself in a pleasure is mere asceticism or self-deprivation for its own sake. To make this a rule of action would not increase the sum of happiness, but reduce it.

In applying the Long-Run Principle, in other words, we must apply it with a certain amount of common sense. We must confine ourselves to consideration of the *relevant* long run, the finite and reasonably *cognizable* long run. This is the grain of truth in Keynes's cynical dictum that "*In the long run* we are all dead."[11] That long run we may no doubt justifiably ignore. We cannot see into eternity.

Yet no future, even the next five minutes, is *certain,* and we cannot do more at any time than act on probabilities (although, as we shall see, some probabilities of a given course of conduct or rule of action are considerably more probable than others). And there are people capable of concern regarding the fate of mankind far beyond the probable length of their own lives.

The Long-Run Principle presents still another problem. This is the value that we ought to attach to future pains and pleasures as compared with present ones. In his list of the seven "circumstances" (or, as he later called them, "elements" or "dimensions") by which we should value a pain or a pleasure, Bentham lists "3. Its *certainty* or *uncertainty,*" and "4. Its *propinquity* or *remoteness.*" Now a remote pain or pleasure is apt to be less certain than a near one; in fact, its uncertainty is widely considered to be a function of its remoteness. But the question we are asking now is to what extent, if any, Bentham was justified in assuming that we ought to attach less value to a remote pain or pleasure than to a near one, even when the element of certainty or uncertainty is disregarded or, as in Bentham's list, treated as a separate consideration.[12]

Most of us cannot prevent ourselves from valuing a future good at less than the same present and otherwise identical good. We value today's dinner, say, more than a similar dinner a year from now. Are we "right" or "wrong" in doing so? It is impossible to answer the question in this form. All of us "undervalue" a future good as compared with a present good. This "undervaluation" is so universal that it may be asked whether it is undervaluation at all. Economically, the value of anything is what it is valued at. It is value *to* somebody. Economic value cannot be thought of apart from a valuer. Is ethical value quite different in kind? Is there such a thing as the "intrinsic" ethical value of a good (as many moralists persist in thinking) apart from anybody's valuation of that good? Here we are concerned merely with the question of how we *ought* to value future goods or satisfactions as compared with present ones.

When we look at the relative value that we actually do assign to them, we find that in the economic world the market has worked out a "rate of interest" which is, in effect, the average or composite rate of discount that the market community applies to future as compared with present goods. When the interest rate is 5 percent, $1.05 a year from now is worth no more than $1 today, or $1 a year from now no more than about 95 cents today. If an individual (who is in desperate need) values $2 a year from now at no more than $1 today, we are perhaps entitled to say that he undervalues future as compared with present goods. But whether we are entitled to say, simply because there *is* a rate of interest or a rate of time-discount, that *the economic community as a whole* "undervalues" the future, is very dubious. Backward communities have a higher rate of future time-discount than progressive communities. The poor tend to put a higher relative valuation on present goods than the rich. But can we say that the lower valuation placed on future as compared with present goods by humanity as a whole is "wrong"?

I for one will no more attempt to answer this question in the ethical than in the economic realm. At best we can judge the individual's valuation against the whole community's valuation. What we can say, however, is that any course of action based on a real underestimation or undervaluation of future consequences will result in less total happiness than one which estimates or values future consequences justly.

The distinction between short- and long-run consequences was implicitly, though not expressly, the basis of the ethical system that Bentham presented in his *Deontology,* in which he classifies all the virtues under the two main heads of Prudence and Beneficence, and further divides them, in four chapters, under the heads of Self-Regarding Prudence, Extra-Regarding Prudence, Negative Efficient Benevolence, and Positive Efficient Benevolence.

It is consideration of long-run consequences that gives Prudence a far larger role in ethics than it has been commonly assumed to have. This is suggested by Bentham's title head, "Extra-Regarding Prudence." The happiness of each of us is dependent upon his fellows. He depends upon their concurrence and cooperation. One can never disregard the happiness of others without running a risk to his own.

To sum up: The distinction between the short-run and the long-run effects of conduct is more valid than the traditional contrasts between the interests of the individual and the interests of society. When the individual acts in his own long-run interests he tends to act also in the long-run interest of the whole society. The longer the run we consider, the more likely are the interests of the individual and of society to become identical. Moral conduct is in the long-run interest of the individual.

To recognize this is to perceive the solution of a basic moral problem that otherwise seems to present a contradiction. The difficulties that arise when this is not clearly recognized can be seen from a passage in an otherwise penetrating writer:

> Moralities are systems of principles whose acceptance by everyone as overruling the dictates of self-interest is in the interest of everyone alike, though following the rules of morality is not of course identical with following self-interest. If it were, there could be no conflict between a morality and self-interest and no point in having rules overriding self-interest. . . . The answer to the question "Why be moral?" is therefore as follows. We should be moral because being moral is following rules designed to overrule self-interest whenever it is in the interest of everyone alike that everyone should set aside his interest.[13]

If we emphasize the distinction between short-run and long-run interests, however, the solution to this problem becomes much simpler and involves no paradox. Then we would rewrite the foregoing passage like this: Moralities are systems of principles whose acceptance by everyone as overruling the apparent dictates of immediate self-interest is in the long-run interest of everyone alike. We should be moral because being moral is following rules which disregard apparent self-interest in the short run and are designed to promote our own real long-run interest as well as the interest of others who are affected by our actions. It is only from a short-sighted view that the interests of the individual appear to be in conflict with those of "society," and vice versa.

Actions or rules of action are not "right" or "wrong" in the sense in which a proposition in physics or mathematics is right or wrong, but expedient or inexpedient, advisable or inadvisable, helpful or harmful. In brief, in ethics the appropriate criterion is not "truth" but *wisdom.* To adopt this concept is, indeed, to return to the concept of the ancients. The moral appeal of Socrates is the appeal to conduct our lives with wisdom. The Proverbs of the Old Testament do not speak dominantly of Virtue or Sin, but of Wisdom and Folly. "Wisdom is the principal thing; therefore get wisdom. . . . The fear of the Lord is the beginning of wisdom. . . . A wise son maketh a glad father: but a foolish son is the heaviness of his mother. . . . As a dog returneth to his vomit, so a fool returneth to his folly."

We shall reserve until later chapters the detailed illustration and application of the Long-Run Principle. Here we are still concerned with the epistemological or theoretical foundations of ethics rather than with casuistry or detailed practical guidance. But it is now possible to take the next step from the theoretical to the practical. It is one of the most important implications of the Long-Run Principle (and one that Bentham, strangely, failed explicitly to recognize) that we must act, not by attempting separately in every case to weigh and compare the probable specific consequences of one moral decision or course of action as against another, but by acting according to some *established general rule or set of rules.* This is what is meant by acting *according to principle.* It is not the consequences (which it is impossible to know in advance) of a specific *act* that we have to consider, but the probable long-run consequences of following a given *rule* of action.

Why this is so, and how it is so, we shall examine in our next chapter.

1. The theme of the present author's *Economics in One Lesson* (New York: Harpers, 1946) is summed up on page 5 as follows: "From this aspect . . . the whole of economics can be reduced to a single lesson, and that lesson can be reduced to a single sentence. *The art of economics consists in looking not merely at the immediate but at the longer effects of any act or policy; it consists in tracing the consequences of that policy not merely for one group but for all groups.*" It is clear that this generalization may be widened to apply to conduct and policy in every field. As applied to ethics it might be stated thus: *Ethics must take into consideration not merely the immediate but the longer effects of any act or rule of action; It must consider the consequences of that act or rule of action not merely for the agent or any particular group but for everybody likely to be affected, presently or in the future, by that act or rule of action.*

2. John Maynard Keynes, *Monetary Reform* (New York: Harcourt Brace, 1924), p. 88.

3. See, however, Ludwig von Mises, *Theory and History* (New Haven: Yale, 1957), pp. 32, 55, 57.

4. Jeremy Bentham, *Morals and Legislation,* Chap. IV., pp. 29–30.

5. Jeremy Bentham, *Deontology,* arranged and edited by John Bowring, 2 vols. (London, 1834), II, 87.

6. Samuel Butler, *Note-Books.*

7. Jeremy Bentham, *Morals and Legislation,* p. 9.

8. *Loc. cit.*

9. *Op. cit.,* p. 8.

10. *Discipline* is also, unfortunately, used in several senses. Thus one meaning given in the *Shorter Oxford English Dictionary* is: "7. Correction; chastisement; in religious use, the mortification of the flesh by penance; also, a beating, or the like." And in *Webster's New International Dictionary* one finds: "7. *R.C.Ch.:* self-inflicted and voluntary corporal punishment, specif., a penitential scourge." But one also finds, in, say, *Webster's Collegiate Dictionary:* "Training which corrects, molds, strengthens, or perfects." This last definition, I think, represents dominant present-day usage.

11. Keynes, *op. cit.,* p. 88. As one who has written a whole book in criticism of Lord Keynes's economic theories (*The Failure of the "New Economics"* [Princeton: Van Nostrand, 1959]), I am bound to point out in justice that this dictum, which is the one for which Lord Keynes is most frequently criticized, was not without warrant in the particular context in which he used it. It is immediately followed by the sentence: "Economists set themselves too easy, too useless a task if in tempestuous seasons they can only tell us that when the storm is long past the ocean is flat again." This is a perfectly valid argument against the neglect of short-run problems and short-run considerations. But the whole trend of Keynes's thinking, as reflected not only in *Monetary Reform* but in his most famous work, *The General*

Theory of Employment, Interest and Money, is to consider only short-run consequences and neglect far more important long-run effects of the policies he proposed.

12. I think I am warranted, from the whole context of his list, in assuming that
Bentham is thinking of what value "the legislator" *ought* to attach to these seven
"dimensions" rather than the value that any given person actually does or that "all"
persons actually do attach to them.

13. Kurt Baier, *The Moral Point of View* (Ithaca, N.Y.: Cornell University
Press, 1958), p. 314.

CHAPTER 5

The Need for General Rules

1. The Contribution of Hume

David Hume, probably the greatest of British philosophers, made three major contributions to ethics. The first was the naming and consistent application of "the principle of utility."[1] The second was his account of sympathy. The third, no less important than the others, was to point out not only that we must adhere inflexibly to *general rules* of action, but *why* this is essential to secure the interests and happiness of the individual and of mankind.

It is a puzzling development in the history of ethical thought, however, that this third contribution has been so often overlooked not only by subsequent writers of the Utilitarian school, including Bentham, but even by historians of ethics when they are discussing Hume himself.[2] One reason for this, perhaps, is that Hume, in the discussion of Morals in his *Treatise of Human Nature* (1740) devotes only a comparatively few paragraphs to the point. And in his *Inquiry Concerning the Principles of Morals,* published twelve years later (in 1752), which in his autobiography he described as "incomparably the best" of all his writings, historical, philosophical, or literary, he gave even less space to it. Yet it is so important and so central that it can hardly receive too much emphasis and elaboration.

In his *Treatise of Human Nature,* Hume observes: "The avidity and partiality of men would quickly bring disorder into the world, if not restrained by some general and inflexible principles. It was therefore with a view to this inconvenience that men have established those principles, and have agreed to restrain themselves by

33

general rules, which are unchangeable by spite and favor, and by particular views of private or public interest."[3]

In his *Inquiry Concerning the Principles of Morals,* a dozen years later, Hume returns to the theme. And it is not till we get to the Appendices that we find any extended discussion, and even this is confined to two or three pages:

> The benefit resulting from [the social virtues of justice and fidelity] is not the consequence of every individual single act, but arises from the whole scheme or system concurred in by the whole or the greater part of the society. General peace and order are the attendants of justice, or a general abstinence from the possessions of others; but a particular regard to the particular right of one individual citizen may frequently, considered in itself, be productive of pernicious consequences. The result of the individual acts is here, in many instances, directly opposite to that of the whole system of actions; and the former may be extremely hurtful, while the latter is, to the highest degree, advantageous. Riches inherited from a parent are in a bad man's hand the instrument of mischief. The right of succession may, in one instance, be hurtful. Its benefit arises only from the observance of the general rule; and it is sufficient if compensation be thereby made for all the ills and inconveniences which flow from particular characters and situations.[4]

Hume then speaks of "the general, inflexible rules necessary to support general peace and order in society," and continues:

> All the laws of nature which regulate property as well as all civil laws are general and regard alone some essential circumstances of the case, without taking into consideration the characters, situations, and connections of the person

concerned or any particular consequences which may result from the determination of these laws in any particular case which offers. They deprive, without scruple, a beneficent man of all his possessions if acquired by mistake, without a good title, in order to bestow them on a selfish miser who has already heaped up immense stores of superfluous riches. Public utility requires that property should be regulated by general inflexible rules; and though such rules are adopted as best serve the same end of public utility, it is impossible for them to prevent all particular hardships or make beneficial consequences result from every individual case. It is sufficient if the whole plan or scheme be necessary to the support of civil society and if the balance of good, in the main, do thereby preponderate much above that of evil.[5]

2. The Principle in Adam Smith

It would be impossible to exaggerate the importance of this principle both in law and in ethics. We will find later that, among other things, it alone can reconcile what is true in some of the traditional controversies of ethics—the long-standing dispute, for example, between Benthamite Utilitarianism and Kantian formalism, between relativism and absolutism, and even between "empirical" and "intuitive" ethics.

Most commentators on Hume completely ignore the point. Even Bentham, who not only took over the principle of utility from Hume, but christened it with the cumbersome name of Utilitarianism, which stuck,[6] missed, for all practical purposes, this vital qualification.

It is only natural that we should look for some trace of the influence of Hume's General-Rules Principle in Adam Smith, his admirer and younger friend (by twelve years), and—at least in some doctrines—his disciple. (Many of the views in *The Wealth of Nations*, on commerce, money, interest, the balance and freedom of trade, taxes and public credit, are anticipated in Hume's *Essays, Literary, Moral, and Political,* published some thirty years earlier.) And we do in fact find that Adam Smith incorporated the General-Rules Principle in his *Theory of the Moral Sentiments* (1759), particularly in Part III, Chapters IV and V. He states it eloquently:

> Our continual observations upon the conduct of others insensibly lead us to form to ourselves certain general rules concerning what is fit and proper either to be done or avoided. . . .[7] The regard to those general rules of conduct is what is properly called a sense of duty, a principle of the greatest consequence in human life, and the only principle by which the bulk of mankind are capable of directing their actions. . . .[8] Without this sacred regard to general rules, there is no man whose conduct can be much depended upon. It is this which constitutes the most essential difference between a man of principle and honor, and a worthless fellow. The one adheres on all occasions steadily and resolutely to his maxims, and preserves through the whole of his life one even tenor of conduct. The other acts variously and accidently, as humour, inclination, or interest chance to be uppermost. . . .[9] Upon the tolerable observance of these duties [justice, truth, chastity, fidelity] depends the very existence of human society, which would crumble into nothing if mankind were not generally impressed with reverence for those important rules of conduct.[10]

But in spite of this emphatic statement of the principle, Adam Smith makes a doubtful qualification which is, in fact, inconsistent with it. He tells us, apparently in contradiction to Hume, that: "We do not originally approve or condemn particular actions because, upon examination, they appear to be agreeable or inconsistent with a certain general rule. The general rule, on the contrary, is formed by finding from experience that all actions of a certain kind, or circumstances in a certain manner, are approved or disapproved of."[11] He goes on to declare that "the man who first saw an inhuman murder committed" would not have to reflect, "in order to conceive how horrible such an action was" that "one of the most sacred rules of conduct" had been violated.[12] And he becomes ironic at the expense of "several very eminent authors" (Hume?) who "draw up their systems in such a manner as if they had supposed that the original judgments of mankind with regard to right and wrong were formed like the decisions of a court of judicatory—by considering first the general rule, and then, secondly, whether the particular action under consideration fell properly within its comprehension."[13]

Smith oversimplifies the problem, and does not recognize his own inconsistency. If we had always, from the beginning of time, instantly recognized, just by seeing them, hearing of them, or doing them, what actions were right and what were wrong, we would not *need* to frame general rules and resolve to abide by general rules, unless it were the general rule: Always do right and never do wrong. We would not even need to study or discuss ethics. We could dispense with all treatises on ethics or even any discussion of specific ethical problems. All ethics could be summed up in the foregoing rule of seven words. Even the Ten Commandments would be nine commandments too many.

3. Rediscovery in the Twentieth Century

The problem, unfortunately, is more complicated. It is true that our present ethical judgments of some actions are instantaneous; they seem based on abhorrence of the act itself, and not on any consideration of its consequences (apart from those that seem inherent in the act, such as the suffering of a person who is being tortured, or the death of a person who is killed), or on any judgment that they involve the violation of an abstract general rule. Nevertheless most of these instantaneous judgments may indeed be partly or mainly based on the fact that a general rule is being violated. We may look with horror on another car speeding directly toward us on *its* left side of the road, though there is nothing *inherently* wrong with driving on the left side of the road, and the whole danger comes from the violation of a general rule. And in our private moral judgments, no less than in law, we do in fact try to decide under what general rule we should act or under what general rule a given act should be classed. The courts must decide whether a given act is First-Degree Murder, or Manslaughter, or Self-Defense. If a patient's disease is hopeless a doctor who is asked for reassurance must decide whether this would be Telling a Lie, or Sparing Needless Suffering. When we are deciding (if we ever consciously do) whether or not to tell our hostess that we can't remember when we have had such a wonderful evening, we must decide whether this would be Perjury, Hypocrisy, or the Duty of Politeness.

The problem of deciding under what rule an act should be classed can sometimes present difficulties. F. H. Bradley was so impressed by these, in fact, that he even deplored any effort to solve the problem "by a reflective deduction" and insisted it must only be done "by an intuitive subsumption, which does not know that it is a subsumption." "No act in the world," he argued, "is without *some* side capable of being subsumed under a good rule; e.g. theft is economy, care for one's relations, protest against bad institutions, really doing oneself but justice, etc.," and *reasoning* about the matter leads straight to immorality (*Ethical Studies,* pp. 196–197). I do not think we need take this obscurantist argument very seriously. Logically followed, it would condemn all reasoning about ethics, including Bradley's. The problem of deciding under what rule of law an act should be classed is one that our courts and judges must solve a thousand times a day, and not by "intuitive subsumption" but by reasoning that will stand up on appeal. In ethics the problem may not often arise—but when it does it is precisely because our "intuitive subsumptions" conflict.

The need of adhering inflexibly to general rules is plain. Even the qualifications to rules must be drawn according to general rules.

An "exception" to a rule must not be capricious, but itself capable of being stated as a rule, capable of being made *part* of a rule, of being *embodied* in a rule. Even here, in brief, we must be guided by generality, predictability, certainty, the non-disappointment of reasonable expectations.

The great principle that Hume discovered and framed was that, while conduct should be judged by its "utility," that is, by its consequences, by its tendency to promote happiness and well-being, it is not specific acts that should be so judged, but general *rules* of action. It is only the probable long-run consequences of these, and not of specific acts, that can reasonably be foreseen. As F. A. Hayek has put it:

> It is true enough that the justification of any particular rule of law must be its usefulness. . . . But, generally speaking, only the rule as a whole must be so justified, not its every application. The idea that each conflict, in law or in morals, should be so decided as would seem most expedient to somebody who could comprehend all the consequences of that decision involves the denial of the necessity of any rules. "Only a society of omniscient individuals could give each person complete liberty to weigh every particular action on general utilitarian grounds." Such an "extreme" utilitarianism leads to absurdity; and only what has been called "restricted" utilitarianism has therefore any relevance to our problem. Yet few beliefs have been more destructive of the respect for the rules of law and of morals than the idea that the rule is binding only if the beneficial effect of observing it in the particular instance can be recognized.[14]

In any case, there will often be a profound difference in our moral judgment, according to which standard we apply. The standards of *direct* or *ad hoc* utilitism will not necessarily in every case be less demanding than the standards of *rule*-utilitism. In fact, to ask a man *in his every act* to do that "which will contribute more than any other act to human happiness" (as some of the older utilitarians did) is to impose upon him an oppressive as well as an impossible choice. For it is impossible for any man to know what all the consequences of a given act will be when it is considered in isolation. It is not impossible for him to know, however, what the probable consequences will be of *following a generally accepted rule.* For these probable consequences are known as a result of the whole of human experience. It is the results of previous human experience that have framed our traditional moral rules. When the individual is asked merely to follow some accepted rule, the moral burdens put upon him are not impossible. The pangs of conscience that may come to him if his action does not turn out to have the most beneficent consequences are not unbearable. For not the least of the advantages of our all acting according to commonly accepted moral rules is that our actions are *predictable* by others and the actions of others are predictable by us, with the result that we are all better able to cooperate with each other in helping each other to pursue our individual ends.

When we judge an act by a mere *ad hoc* utilitism, it is as if we asked: What would be the consequences of this act *if* it could be considered as an isolated act, as a *just-this-once* act, without consequences as a *precedent* or as an *example to others?* But this means that we are deliberately disregarding what may be its most important consequences.

In pursuing the further implications of the principle of acting according to general rules, we must consider the whole relationship of ethics and law.

---

1. Some of Hume's doctrines were anticipated by Shaftesbury (1671–1713) and still more clearly by Hutcheson (1694–1747), the real author of the "Benthamite" dictum that "that action is best which procures the greatest happiness for the greatest numbers." But Hume was the first to name the principle of "utility" and to make it the basis of his system. Though, unlike Bentham, Hume seldom gave an explicitly hedonistic implication to "utility," he wrote one paragraph,

beginning: "The chief spring or actuating principle of the human mind is pleasure or pain" (*A Treatise of Human Nature,* (1740), Book III, Part III, sec. 1), that may have been the inspiration of the famous opening paragraph of Bentham's *Morals and Legislation.*

2. It is even more ironic that contemporary philosophers who have rediscovered or adopted the principle, under the name of *rule-utilitarianism,* seem to be unaware of Hume's explicit statement of it. Thus John Hospers writes in *Human Conduct* (New York: Harcourt, Brace, & World, 1961, p. 318): "*Rule-Utilitarianism* is a distinctively twentieth-century amendment of the utilitarianism of Bentham and Mill." And Richard B. Brandt (in *Ethical Theory,* 1959, p. 396) writes: "This theory, a product of the last decade, is not a novel one. We find statements of it in J. S. Mill and John Austin in the nineteenth century; and indeed we find at least traces of it much earlier, in discussions of the nature and function of law by the early Greeks." But he does not mention Hume.

3. David Hume, *A Treatise of Human Nature,* Book III, Part II, sec. 6.

4. David Hume, "Of Political Society" in *An Inquiry Concerning the Principles of Morals* (1751) (New York: Library of Liberal Arts: 1957), Sec. IV, p. 40; "Some Further Considerations with Regard to Justice," Appendix III, p. 121.

5. *Ibid.,* p. 122.

6. Bentham plays an immense role in the history of ideas since the eighteenth century, and his numerous verbal coinages made permanent additions to the language without which modern discussion could hardly get along. His most famous coinage was *international.* But he also gave us *codification, maximize,* and *minimize,* and many words of more limited usefulness, like *cognoscible* and *cognoscibility.* But he did an ill service to mankind when he invented *Utilitarian* and *Utilitarianism,* which simply pile up needless and inexcusable syllables.

Everything began, quietly enough, with Hume, with the English adjective *useful* and the English abstract noun *utility,* derived respectively from the latin *utilis* and *utilitas* through the French *utilité.* Why not, then, simply *Utilist* as the adjective for the doctrine, and the noun for the writer holding the doctrine, and simply *Utilism,* or at most *Utilitism,* as the name of the doctrine? But no. Instead of beginning with the adjective, Bentham began with the longer abstract Latin noun made from the adjective. Then he added three syllables—*arian*—to the noun to turn it back into an adjective. Then he added another syllable—*ism*—to turn the inflated adjectitve made from an abstract noun back into another abstract noun. Now behold the eight-syllabled sesquipedalian monstrosity, *Utilitarianism.* Then John Stuart Mill came along and nailed the thing down by making the name the title of his famous essay. So as the name for the doctrine as it has existed historically, posterity is stuck with the word. But perhaps from now on, when we are describing doctrines not identical with historic *Utilitarianism,* as developed by Bentham and Mill, but involving the doctrine that duty and virtue are means to an end rather than sufficient ends in themselves, we can use the word *Teleology* or *Teleotism* or the simpler words *utilic, Utilist* and *Utilitism.* Thus we save three syllables, and escape from some confusing and outmoded associations.

7. *Adam Smith's Moral and Political Philosophy,* ed. Herbert W. Schneider (New York: Hafner Publishing Co., 1948), p. 185.

8. *Ibid.,* p. 189.

9. *Ibid.,* p. 190.

10. *Ibid.,* p. 191.

11. *Ibid.,* p. 186.

12. *Loc. cit.*

13. *Ibid.,* p. 187.

14. F. A. Hayek, *The Constitution of Liberty* (Chicago: University of Chicago Press, 1960), p. 159.

CHAPTER 6

Ethics and Law

1. Natural Law

In primitive societies religion, morals, law, customs, manners, exist as an undifferentiated whole.[1] The boundaries between them are hazy and ill-defined. Their respective provinces are distinguished only gradually. For generations it is not only ethics that retains a theological base, but jurisprudence, which was a part of theology for two centuries prior to the Reformation.

The outstanding illustration of the fusing and separation of the provinces of ethics, law, and theology is the growth of the doctrine of Natural Law. The Greeks put a theoretical moral foundation under law by the doctrine of natural right. The Roman jurists made natural right into natural law and sought to discover the content of this natural law and to declare it. The Middle Ages put a theological foundation under natural law. The seventeenth and eighteenth centuries took out this theological foundation and replaced it, or partially replaced it, by a rational foundation. At the end of the eighteenth century Kant tried to replace the rational foundation by a metaphysical foundation.[2]

But what was natural law, and how did the concept arise? In the hands of Roman lawyers, the Greek theories of what was *right* by nature and what was *right* by convention or enactment gave rise to a distinction between law by nature and law by custom or enactment. Rules based on reason *were* law by nature. The right or the just by nature became law by nature or natural law. In this way began the identification of the legal with the moral that has been characteristic of natural-law thinkers ever since.[3]

In the Middle Ages the concept of natural law was identified with the concept of divine law. Natural law proceeded immediately from reason but ultimately from God. According to Thomas Aquinas, it was a reflection of the "reason of the divine wisdom governing the whole universe." Later thinkers saw no conflict between natural law and divine law. According to Grotius, for example, both were based on eternal reason and on the will of God who wills only reason. This is also the view of Blackstone. It is reflected in the views of American judges, as, for example, Mr. Justice Wilson, who tells us that God "is under the glorious necessity of not contradicting himself."[4]

The concept of natural law has played a major role both in legal confusion and in legal progress. The confusion comes from its unfortunate name. When natural law is identified with the "laws of nature" it comes to be assumed that human thought can have no part in forming or creating it. It is assumed to pre-exist. It is the function of our reason merely to discover it. In fact, many writers on natural law throw out reason altogether. It is not necessary. We know—or at least *they* know—just what natural law is from direct intuition.

This aroused the wrath of Bentham. He contended that the doctrine of natural law was merely one of the "contrivances for avoiding the obligation of appealing to any external standard, and for prevailing upon the reader to accept of the author's sentiment or opinion as a reason for itself. . . . A great multitude of people are continually talking of the Law of Nature; and then they go on giving you their sentiments about what is right and what is wrong: and these sentiments, you are to understand, are so many chapters and sections of the Law of Nature. . . . The fairest and openest of them all is that sort of man who speaks out, and says, I am of the number of the Elect: now God himself takes care to inform the Elect what is right: and that with so good effect, and let them strive ever so, they cannot help not only knowing it but practising it. If therefore a man wants to know what is right and what is wrong, he has nothing to do but to come to me."[5]

If, however, we think of natural law as merely a misnomer for Ideal Law, or Law-as-It-Ought-to-Be, and if, in addition, we have the humility or scientific caution to assume that we do not intuitively or automatically know what this is, but that it is something to be discovered and formulated by experience and reason, and that we can constantly improve our concepts without ever reaching finality or perfection, then we have a powerful tool for the continuous reform of positive law. This, in fact, was the implicit assumption and method of Bentham himself.

2. The Common Law

Positive law and "positive" morality are both products of a long historical growth. They grew together, as part of an undifferentiated tradition and custom that included religion. But law tended to become secular and independent of theology sooner than did ethics. It also became more definite and explicit. Anglo-American common law, in particular, grew through customs of judicial decision. Individual judges realized, implicitly if not explicitly, that law and the application of law must be certain, uniform, predictable. They tried to solve individual cases upon their "merits"; but they recognized that their decision in one case must be "consistent" with their decision in another, and that the decisions of one court must be consistent with those of others, so that they would not easily be overthrown on appeal.

They therefore sought for general rules under which particular cases might be brought and decided. To find these general rules they looked for analogies both in their own previous decisions and in the previous decisions of other courts. Contending lawyers usually did not deny the existence or validity of these general rules. They did not deny that cases should be decided in accordance with established precedents. But they tried to find and to cite the analogies and precedents that favored their particular side. The attorney for one litigant would argue that his client's case was analogous to previous case Y, not X, and that it therefore came under Rule B, not Rule A, while the attorney for the opposing litigant would argue the opposite.

Thus there grew up, through precedent and analogical reasoning, the great body of the Common Law. There was in it, of course, in the beginning, much reverence for mere precedent as such, whether the precedent was rational or irrational. But there was clearly a great deal of utilic rationality in respecting precedent as such: this tended to make the application of law certain, uniform, and predictable. Moreover, there was also, even in early periods, and increasingly later, an element of utilic rationality in particular decisions. For even in trying to decide a case "upon its individual merits," a judge would probably give at least one eye to a consideration not only of the probable practical effects of that particular decision but also to the probable practical effects of like decisions in other cases. Thus the Common Law was built up both through induction and deduction: in deciding particular cases judges arrived at general rules, i.e., at rules that would apply to like cases; and when a new concrete case came before them, they would look for the relevant pre-existing general rule under which it would be appropriate and just to decide it.

Thus judges both made law and applied it. But common law had the defect of a wide margin of uncertainty. Where precedents were conflicting and analogies were debatable, litigants could not know in advance by which precedent or analogy a particular judge would be guided. Where the general rule or principle had received vague or inconsistent statement, no one could know in advance which form of the rule a given judge would accept as valid or determining. How could men protect themselves from capricious or arbitrary decisions? How could they know in advance whether the actions they were taking were legal or whether the contracts and agreements they were making would be called valid? The demand arose for a more explicit written law.

But the law as a whole, common and statute law together, was a steadily growing and constantly more consistent body of general rules, and even of general-rules-for-finding-the-general-rule under which a particular case came. And the attempt to make these general rules more precise and consistent, and to find a utilitarian basis for them or reconstruct them on such a basis, led to the development of the philosophy of law and the science of jurisprudence. Writers on jurisprudence were divided roughly into two schools, the analytical and the philosophical. "Analytical jurisprudence broke with philosophy and with ethics completely. . . . The ideal pattern of the analytical jurist was one of a logically consistent and logically interdependent system of legal precepts. . . . Assuming an exact logically defined separation of powers, the analytical jurist contended that law and morals were distinct and unrelated and that he was concerned only with law."[6] On the other hand, "Throughout the nineteenth century philosophical jurists devoted much of their attention to the relation of law to morals, the relation of jurisprudence to ethics."[7]

Yet there is an irony here. While most writers on jurisprudence have been constantly concerned with the relations of law to ethics, while they have sought to make legal rules consistent with ethical requirements, and to find what jurisprudence has to learn from ethics, moralists have not at all troubled to find what they could learn from jurisprudence. For the jurists have made the tacit assumption that while the law is something that was created and developed by man, and is to be perfected by him, ethics is something already created by God and known to man by intuition. The great majority of ethical writers have made a similar assumption. Even the evolutionary and utilitarian moralists have not troubled to see what they could learn from a study of law and jurisprudence.

And this was true, strangest of all, even of Jeremy Bentham, who made tremendous contributions both to jurisprudence and to ethics, and whose most famous book is called, significantly, *Introduction to the Principles of Morals and Legislation*. Yet he too was concerned principally with what legislation had to learn from morals, or rather with what both had to learn from the Principle of Utility or the Greatest Happiness Principle, and not with the great lesson that ethical philosophy had to learn from jurisprudence and law—the importance and necessity of general rules.

Nevertheless, Bentham has left us an illuminating simile: "Legislation is a circle with the same center as moral philosophy, but its circumference is smaller."[8] And Jellinek in 1878 subsumed law under morals in the same way by declaring that law was a minimum ethics. It was only a part of morals—the part that had to do with the indispensable conditions of the social order. The remainder of morals, desirable but not indispensable, he called "an ethical luxury."[9]

3. The Relativism of Anatole France

The great lesson that moral philosophy has to learn from legal philosophy is the necessity for adhering to general rules. It also has to learn the nature of these rules. They must be general, certain, uniform, regular, predictable, and equal in their application. "Rules of property, rules as to commercial transactions, the rules that maintain the security of acquisitions and the security of transactions in a society of complex economic organization—such rules may be and ought to be of general and absolute application."[10] "The very conception of law involves ideas of uniformity, regularity, predictability."[11]

The essential requirements of law have seldom been better described than by F. A. Hayek in *The Constitution of Liberty.* It must be free from arbitrariness, privilege, or discrimination. It must apply to all, and not merely to particular persons or groups. It must be certain. It must consist in the enforcement of known rules. These rules must be general and abstract rather than specific and concrete. They must be so clear that court decisions are predictable. In brief, the law must be certain, general, and equal.[12] "The true contrast to a reign of status is the reign of general and equal laws, of the rules which are the same for all."[13] "As they operate through the expectations that they create, it is essential that they be always applied, irrespective of whether or not the consequences in a particular instance seem desirable."[14] True laws must be "known and certain. . . . The essential point is that the decisions of the courts can be predicted."[15]

When these requirements are met, the requirements of liberty are met. As John Locke put it: "The end of the law is, not to abolish or restrain, but to preserve and enlarge freedom. . . . For liberty is to be free from restraint and violence from others, which cannot be where there is no law."[16]

"Freedom of men under government is to have a standing rule to live by, common to every one of that society, and made by the legislative power erected in it; a liberty to follow my own will in all things, where that rule prescribes not: and not to be subject to the inconstant, uncertain, arbitrary will of another man."[17]

When Justice is represented on courthouse statues as being blind, it does not mean that she is blind to the justice of the case, but blind to the wealth, social position, sex, color, looks, amiability or other qualities of the particular litigants. It means that she recognizes that justice, happiness, peace, and order can only be established, in the long run, by respect for general rules, rather than respect for the "merits" of each particular case. This is what Hume means when he insists that justice will often require that a poor good man be forced to pay money to a rich bad man—if, for example, it concerns the payment of a just debt. And this is what the advocates of an *ad hoc* "justice," a "justice" that regards only the specific "merits" of the particular case before the court, without considering what the extension of the rule of that decision would imply, have never understood. Almost the whole weight of the novelists and intellectuals of the last two centuries, in their treatment of both legal and moral questions, has been thrown in this *ad hoc* direction. Their attitude is summed up in the famous ironical jibe by Anatole France at "the majestic equality of the law that forbids the rich as well as the poor to sleep under bridges, to beg in the streets and to steal bread."[18]

But neither Anatole France nor any of those who take this *ad hoc* view have ever bothered to say what rules or guides, apart from their own immediate feelings, they would apply in place of equality before the law. Would they decide in each case of theft how much the thief "needed" the particular thing he stole, or how little its rightful owner "needed" it? Would they make it illegal only for a rich man to steal from a poor man? Legal for anybody to steal from anybody richer than himself? Would Anatole France himself, in his pose of magnanimity, have considered it all right for anyone to pirate or plagiarize from him, provided only that the plagiarist could show that he was not yet as prosperous or well-known as Anatole France?

The forthright declaration of a Thomas Huxley that it is not only illegal but immoral for a man to steal a loaf of bread even if he is starving, seems like a cruel and shocking Victorian pronouncement to all our "modern" ethical relativists, to all the *ad hoc* theoreticians who pride themselves on their peculiar "compassion." But they have never suggested what rules should be put in place of the general rules they deplore, or how the exceptions should be determined. The only general rule they do in fact seem to have in mind is one they seldom dare to utter—that each man should be a law unto himself, that each man should decide for himself, for example, whether his "need" is great enough or the "need" of his intended victim small enough to justify a particular contemplated theft.

4. Inner and Outer Circle

Before concluding this discussion of the relation of law to ethics, let us turn back to the simile from Bentham that law is a circle with the same center as moral philosophy but with a smaller circumference, and to the similar conclusion of Jellinek that law is a "minimum ethics." Let us try to see just where the radius of the smaller legal circle ends, and why it ends there.

We may do this by a few concrete illustrations. The first is of the schoolmaster who said: "Boys, be pure in heart or I'll flog you."[19] The point is that the law can only operate through sanctions— through punishment, redress, or forcible prevention—and therefore can only insure the outward morality of words and acts.

The second illustration is that of an athletic young man with a rope and a life belt at hand, who sits on a bench in a park along a river bank, and quietly sees a child drown, although he could act without the least danger.[20] The law has refused to impose liability. As Ames has put it: "He took away nothing from a person in jeopardy, he simply failed to confer a benefit upon a stranger. . . . The law does not compel active benevolence between man and man. It is left to one's conscience whether he will be the good Samaritan or not."[21]

This legal reasoning is supported, also, by certain practical difficulties of proof. Suppose there is more than one man watching on the bank, and each contends that the other is in a much better position to effect the rescue? Or suppose we take the broader question raised by Dean Pound: "If John Doe is helpless and starving, shall he sue Henry Ford or John D. Rockefeller?"[22] This raises the question of the difficulty of saying upon whom the duty of being the Good Samaritan should devolve.

But if we pass over these practical difficulties, and come back to our original illustration of the man who sits alone on a bank and coolly lets a child drown, knowing there is no other person from whom help can come but himself, there can be no question of what the common sense moral judgment upon his act would be. The case is sufficient to illustrate the far wider sphere of ethics as compared with law.[23] Morality certainly calls for active benevolence beyond that called for by the law.

1. See Roscoe Pound, *Law and Morals* (Chapel Hill, N.C.: University of North Carolina Press, 1926), pp. 26, 85, and *passim.* This is an especially valuable discussion not only for its analysis but for its scholarship. It contains a bibliography of 24 pages.

2. *Ibid.,* p. 12.

3. *Ibid.,* pp. 6–7.

4. *Ibid.,* pp. 8–9.

5. Jeremy Bentham, *Morals and Legislation,* pp. 17 and 18 (6,9).

6. Roscoe Pound, *op. cit.,* pp. 40, 41, 43.

7. *Ibid.,* p. 85.

8. I find this quoted in Albert Schweitzer, *The Philosophy of Civilization* (New York: Macmillan, 1957), p. 157, but have been unable to trace it down, in these words, in either Bentham's *Morals and Legislation,* the *Deontology,* or *A Fragment on Government.*

9. Jellinek, *Die sozialethische Bedeutung von Recht, Unrecht und der Strafe,* 1878 (2nd ed., 1908), Chaps. 1 and 2. See also Pound, *op. cit.,* p. 103.

10. Roscoe Pound, *op. cit.,* p. 71.

11. *Ibid.,* p. 79.

12. F. A. Hayek, *The Constitution of Liberty,* Chaps. 10, 11, and 12.

13. *Ibid.,* p. 154.

14. *Ibid.,* p. 158.

15. *Ibid.,* p. 208.

16. John Locke, *Second Treatise of Civil Government,* (1689) Sec. 57.

17. *Ibid.,* Sec. 21.

18. Anatole France, *Le Lys rouge* (Paris, 1894), p. 117.

19. Sir Frederick Pollock, *First Book of Jurisprudence,* (4th ed.), p. 47n.

20. Roscoe Pound, *op. cit.,* pp. 68–69.

21. Ames, "Law and Morals," in 22 *Harv. Law Rev.* 97, 112 (1909).

22. Roscoe Pound, *op. cit.,* p. 68.

23. But Bentham asks, in *Morals and Legislation* (1780), p. 323: "Why should it not be made the duty of every man to save another from mischief, when it can be done without prejudicing himself, as well as to abstain from bringing it on to him?" And he adds in a footnote: "A woman's head-dress catches fire; water is at hand; a man, instead of assisting to quench the fire, looks on, and laughs at it. A drunken man, falling with his face downwards into a puddle, is in danger of suffocation; lifting his head a little on one side would save him; another man sees this and lets him lie. A quantity of gunpowder is scattered about a room; a man is going into it with a lighted candle; another, knowing this, lets him go in without warning. Who is there that in any of these cases would think punishment misapplied?"

CHAPTER 7

Traffic Rules and Moral Rules

We may illustrate and reinforce the comparison in the last chapter between ethics and law by taking what may seem at first glance a trivial example—the necessity of framing, enforcing, and adhering to traffic rules.

A closer look will show, I think, that the illustration is not trivial. In present-day America, and even in Europe, it represents the citizen's most frequent contact with the law. It calls for the strictest daily, hourly, and even moment-to-moment observance of prescribed rules, impartially enforced on all.

It is instructive to notice that Hume, insisting even in the middle of the eighteenth century on "the necessity of rules wherever men have any intercourse with each other," went on to point out: "They cannot even pass each other on the road without rules. Wagoners, coachmen, and postilions have principles by which they give the way; and these are chiefly founded on mutual ease and convenience."[1]

Now the first thing to be observed about traffic rules is that they illustrate with special force John Locke's principle that "The end of the law is, not to abolish or restrain, but to preserve and enlarge freedom."[2] They do not exist in order to reduce or to slow up traffic, but to accelerate and maximize it to the greatest extent consistent with mutual safety. Red lights are not put up so that people will be compelled to stop in front of them. The lights and rules do not exist for their own sakes. They exist to provide the freest and smoothest flow of traffic, and to reduce conflicts, accidents, and disputes to a minimum.

True, the traffic rules rest in part on decisions that are arbitrary (though these "arbitrary" decisions usually grow out of immemorial custom). It may be originally a matter of indifference whether we decide that cars should pass each other on the right, as in the United States and most other countries, or on the left, as in England. But *once the rule is fixed,* once it is certain and known, it is of the utmost importance that everyone conform to it. In traffic-rule enforcement, as in much wider areas of law and morals, we cannot allow the right of private judgment. We cannot allow every individual to decide for himself, for example, whether it is better to drive on the right or on the left side of the road. Here is an example of a rule that must be obeyed *simply because it has already been established,* simply because it *is* the accepted rule.

And this principle has the widest bearings. We do and should obey rules, in law, manners and morals, simply because they *are* the established rules. This is their utility. We cooperate better in helping to achieve each other's ends by acting on rules *on which others can count.* We cooperate by being able to *rely* on each other, by being able to *anticipate with confidence* what the other fellow is going to do. And we can have this essential mutual confidence and reliance only if both of us act in accordance with the established rule and each knows that the other is going to act in accordance with the established rule. When two drivers are coming straight towards each other, each driving at a mile a minute near the middle of a narrow country road, each must know that the other, soon enough before the moment of passage, is going to bear toward and pass on the right (or in England on the left) as the established rule prescribes.

In short, in ethics as in law, the traditional and accepted rule is to be followed *unless there are clear and strong reasons against it.* The burden of proof is never on the established rule, but on breaking or changing the rule. And even if the rule is defective it may be unwise for the individual to ignore it or defy it unless he can hope to get it *generally* changed.

Each moral rule must be judged, of course, in accordance with its utility. But some moral rules have this utility simply because they are already accepted. In any case, this established acceptance *adds* to the utility of rules that have utility on other grounds.

It is the task of the moral philosopher, and even of the rule-utilitist, not so much to *frame* the appropriate moral rule governing a particular situation as to *find* the appropriate moral rule. In this he is similar to a judge finding and interpreting the relevant law. The fallacy of too many moral philosophers, ancient and modern, has been the assumption that we can begin *ab initio,* tear up all the existing ethical rules by the roots, or ignore them and start fresh. This would be obviously silly and impossible when dealing, for example, with language. It is no less silly, and far more dangerous, to try to do the same with established moral codes which, like languages, are the product of immemorial social evolution. The improvement or perfection of moral codes, like the improvement or perfection of languages, is to be achieved by piecemeal reforms.

It has been observed again and again how the morality of savage tribes decays and disintegrates when they are confronted by the utterly alien moral code of their "civilized" conquerors. They lose respect for their old moral code before they acquire respect for the new one. They acquire only the vices of civilization. The moral philosophers who have preached root-and-branch substitution, in accordance with some "new" ill-digested and oversimplified principle, have had the effect of undermining existing morality, of creating skepticism and indifference, and of making the rules by which the individual acts "a matter of personal taste."

The traffic-rule illustration throws light also on the philosophy of utilitarianism. Naive hedonism or crude utilitarianism would tell you to do whatever gave you most pleasure at the moment. If you could get to your destination fastest in a particular case by passing red lights without accident and without getting caught, that is what you should do. But a truly enlightened utilitism would insist that it is only by everyone's adhering strictly to general traffic rules that the smoothest and fullest traffic flow, the fewest disputes and accidents, and the maximum satisfaction of drivers, can be achieved in the long run.

We have a still further lesson to learn from the analogy of traffic rules. In general, as with moral rules, we must adhere inflexibly to them. True, expediency and even long-run utility require that there must sometimes be exceptions. *But even the exceptions must be governed by rules.* For example, fire-engines, police-cars, and ambulances are allowed to go through traffic lights. *But only under certain specified conditions.* The fire-engine must be going to a fire, not coming from it. The police car must be in hot pursuit of criminals or responding to an emergency call for help. The ambulance must also be responding to an emergency call. And even the exceptions we allow, it must be recognized, are not without their danger—to pedestrians, to cross-street traffic, to the fire-engine, police car, or ambulance occupants themselves.

None of these exceptions, moreover, means that anybody is free to pass a red light because he is a public official, or a Very Important Person, or considers stopping inconvenient. In the same way, and for the same reason, no one is free to flout the moral law because he considers himself a superman. If a driver were asked, "Why did you pass that red light?" and he replied, "Because I am a genius," the humor and effrontery would not be more than that of the Nietzsches and Oscar Wildes and whole droves of self-styled "Non-Conformists" with their claims to be beyond morality. If rules are not universally and inflexibly obeyed, they lose their utility. To quote Locke once more, "Liberty is to be free from restraint and violence from others, which cannot be where there is no law."[3]

Still one more lesson is to be learned from the analogy of traffic rules—or perhaps it is merely the restatement of previous lessons in another form. One of the purposes of traffic rules, like one of the purposes of all law and all morals, is to learn *how to keep out of each other's way.* In traffic each of us may have a different destination, as in life each may have a different goal. That is one reason why we must all adhere to a set of general rules which not only avert head-on collisions, but enable each other to get to our destinations sooner. Traffic rules, like legal and moral rules in general, are not adopted for their own sakes. They are not adopted primarily to restrain but to liberate. They are adopted to *minimize* frustration and suppression in the long run, and to maximize the satisfactions of all and therefore of each.

The traffic rules are, in sum, a legal system and a moral system in microcosm. Their specific purpose is to maximize traffic and to maximize safety, to enable each to reach his destination with the least interference from others. Whenever paths cross or conflict, *somebody* must yield the right of way to somebody else. I must sometimes give way to you, and you must sometimes give way to me. These times must be unambiguously and unmistakably determined by some general rule or set of general rules. (In traffic rules, traffic from the side streets must give precedence to traffic on the main avenues, or the car on the left must yield to the car on the right.) But who has the right of way is determined not by who you are, or who the other fellow is, but by the *objective situation,* or by a situation that can be objectively defined.

And so the traffic laws embody and illustrate one of the broadest principles of law and morals. As one writer on law puts it: "The problem consists in allowing such an exercise of each personal will as is compatible with the exercise of other wills. . . . A law is a limitation of one's freedom of action for the sake of avoiding collision with others. . . . In social life, as we know, men have not only to avoid collisions, but to arrange cooperation in all sorts of ways, and the one common feature of all these forms of cooperation is the limitation of individual wills in order to achieve a common purpose."[4]

And as Dean Pound, summarizing the view of Kant, writes: "The problem of the law is to keep conscious free-willing beings from interference with each other. It is so to order them that each shall exercise his freedom in a way consistent with the freedom of all

others, since all others are to be regarded equally as ends in themselves."[5]

1. David Hume, *An Inquiry Concerning the Principles of Morals*, Sec. IV, p. 40.

2. John Locke, *Second Treatise of Civil Government,* Sec. 57.

3. *Loc. cit.*

4. Paul Vinogradoff, *Common-Sense in Law* (New York: Henry Holt, 1914), pp. 46–47.

5. Roscoe Pound, *Law and Morals,* p. 97.

CHAPTER 8

Morals and Manners

Let us recall once more that in primitive societies religion, morals, law, customs, manners exist as an undifferentiated whole. We cannot say with confidence which came first. They came together. It is only in comparatively modern times that they have become clearly differentiated from each other; and as they have done so, they have developed different traditions.

Nowhere is this difference in tradition more striking than in that between religious ethics and manners. Too often moral codes, especially those still largely attached to religious roots, are ascetic and grim. Codes of manners, on the other hand, usually require us to be at least outwardly cheerful, agreeable, gracious, convivial—in short, a contagious source of cheer to others. So far, in some respects, has the gap between the two traditions widened, that a frequent theme of plays and novels in the eighteenth and nineteenth centuries and even today is the *contrast* between the rough diamond, the crude proletarian or peasant with inflexible honesty and a heart of gold, and the suave, polished lady or gentleman with perfect manners but completely amoral and with a heart of ice.

The overemphasis on this contrast has been unfortunate. It has prevented most writers on ethics from recognizing that both manners and morals rest on the same underlying principle. That principle is *sympathy, kindness, consideration for others.*

It is true that a part of any code of manners is merely conventional and arbitrary, like knowing which fork to use for the salad, but the heart of every code of manners lies much deeper. Manners developed, not to make life more complicated and awkward (though elaborately ceremonial manners do), but to make it in the long run smoother and simpler—a dance, and not a series of bumps and jolts. The extent to which it does this is the test of any code of manners.

Manners are minor morals. Manners are to morals as the final sandpapering, rubbing, and polishing on a fine piece of furniture are to the selection of the wood, the sawing, chiseling, and fitting. They are the finishing touch.

Emerson is one of the few modern writers who have explicitly recognized the ethical basis of manners. "Good manners," he wrote, "are made up of petty sacrifices.

Let us pursue this aspect of manners a little further. Manners, as we have seen, consist in consideration for others. They consist in deferring to others. One tries to deal with others with unfailing courtesy. One tries constantly to spare the feelings of others. It is bad manners to monopolize the conversation, to talk too much about oneself, to boast, because all this irritates others. It is good manners to be modest, or at least to appear so, because this pleases others. It is good manners for the strong to yield to the weak, the well to the sick, the young to the old.

Codes of manners, in fact, have set up an elaborate, unwritten, but well understood order of precedence, which serves in the realm of politeness like the traffic rules we considered in the preceding chapter. This order of precedence is, in fact, a set of "traffic rules" symbolized in the decision concerning who goes first through a doorway. The gentleman yields to the lady; the younger yields to the older; the able-bodied yield to the ill or the crippled; the host yields to the guest. Sometimes these categories are mixed, or other considerations prevail, and then the rule becomes unclear. But the unwritten code of rules laid down by good manners in the long run saves time rather than consumes it, and tends to take the minor jolts and irritations out of life.

The truth of this is most likely to be recognized whenever manners deteriorate. "My generation of radicals and breakers-down," wrote Scott Fitzgerald to his daughter, "never found anything to take the place of the old virtues of work and courage and the old graces of courtesy and politeness."

Ceremony can be overelaborate and therefore time-consuming, tiring, and boring, but without any ceremony life would be barren, graceless, and brutish. Nowhere is this truth more clearly recognized than in the moral code of Confucius: "Ceremonies and music should not for a moment be neglected by any one. . . . The instructive and transforming power of ceremonies is subtle. They check depravity before it has taken form, causing men daily to move toward what is good and to keep themselves from wrong-doing, without being conscious of it. . . . Ceremonies and music in their nature resemble Heaven and earth, penetrate the virtues of the spiritual intelligences, bring down spirits from above and lift the souls that are abased."[1]

To recognize the truth of this, we have only to imagine how bare and empty life would seem to many without marriage ceremonies, funeral ceremonies, christenings, and Sunday church services. This is the great appeal of religion to many who give a very tepid credence to the dogmas on which their religion is ostensibly founded.

In the ethics of Confucius manners play a major role, as they should. I do not know of any modern philosopher who has deliberately sought to base his ethical system on a widening and idealization of the traditional code of manners, but the effort would probably prove instructive, and *prima facie* less foolish than one rooted in some idealization of asceticism and self-abasement.

I have said that manners are minor ethics. But in another sense they are major ethics, because they are, in fact, the ethics of everyday life. Every day and almost every hour of our lives, those of us who are not hermits or anchorites have an opportunity to practice the minor ethics of good manners, of kindness toward and consideration for others in little things, of petty sacrifices. It is only on great and rare occasions of life that most of us have either the need or the opportunity to practice what I may call Heroic Ethics. Yet most ethical writers seem to be almost exclusively concerned with heroic ethics, with Nobility, Magnanimity, All-Embracing Love, Saintliness, Self-Sacrifice. And they despise any effort to frame or to find the rules or even to seek the rationale behind the workaday ethics for the masses of humanity.

We need to be more concerned with *everyday* morality and relatively less with *crisis* morality. If ethical treatises were more concerned with everyday morality they would stress far more than they do the importance of good manners, of politeness, of consideration for others in little things (a habit which must carry over into larger things). They would praise the day-to-day social cooperation that consists in doing one's own job conscientiously, efficiently, and cheerfully.

Most writers on ethics, however, still *contrast* manners and morals rather than treat them as complementary. There is no more frequent character in modern fiction than the man or woman with suave and polished manners and all the outward show of politeness but completely cold, calculating, selfish and even sometimes fiendish at heart. Such characters exist, but they are the exception, not the rule. They are less frequently found than their opposites— the upright, honest, and even kind-hearted person who is often unintentionally blunt or even rude, and "rubs people the wrong way." The existence of both classes of persons is in part the result of the existence in separate compartments of the tradition of morals and the tradition of good breeding. Moralists have too often tended to treat etiquette as of no particular importance, or even as irrelevant to morals. The code of good breeding, especially the code of the "gentleman, was for a long period largely a class code. The "gentleman's" code applied mainly to his relations with other gentlemen, not with his "inferiors." He paid his "debts of honor," for example—his gambling debts—but not his debts to poor tradesmen. Notwithstanding the special and far from trivial duties sometimes imposed by *noblesse oblige,* the code of good breeding, as it existed in the eighteenth and nineteenth centuries, did not necessarily exclude a sometimes cruel snobbery.

But the defects in the conventional code of morals and in the conventional code of manners are corrected when the two traditions are fused—when the code of manners is treated as, in effect, an extension of the code of morals.

It is sometimes supposed that the two codes dictate different actions. The traditional code of ethics is thought to teach that one should always tell the exact and literal truth. The tradition of good breeding, on the other hand, puts its emphasis on sparing the feelings of others, and even on pleasing them at the cost of the exact truth.

A typical example concerns the tradition of what you say to your host and hostess on leaving a dinner party. You congratulate them, say, on a wonderful dinner, and add that you do not know when you have had a more enjoyable evening. The exact and literal truth may be that the dinner was mediocre, or worse, and that the evening was only moderately enjoyable or a downright bore. Nevertheless, provided your exaggerations and protestations of pleasure are not so awkward or extreme that they sound insincere or ironic, the course you have taken is in accord with the dictates of morality no less than with those of etiquette. Nothing is gained by hurting other people's feelings, not to speak of arousing ill will against yourself, to no purpose. Technically, you may have told an untruth. But as your parting remarks are the accepted, conventional and expected thing, they are not a lie. Your host and hostess, moreover, have not really been deceived; they know that your praise and thanks are in accordance with a conventional and practically universal code, and they have no doubt taken your words at the appropriate discount.

The same considerations apply to all the polite forms of correspondence—the dear-sir's, the yours-truly's, and yours-sincerely's, and even, until not so long ago, the your-humble-servant's. It is centuries since these forms were taken seriously and literally. But their omission would be a deliberate and unnecessary rudeness, frowned upon alike by the codes both of manners and morals.

A rational morality also recognizes that there are exceptions to the principle that one should always tell the full literal and exact truth. Should a plain girl be told that, because of her plainness, she is unlikely to find a husband? Should a pregnant mother be told at once that her eldest child has been killed in an accident? Should a man who may not know it be told that he is hopelessly dying of cancer? There are occasions when it may be necessary to utter such truths; there are occasions when they may and should be withheld or concealed. The rule of truth-telling, on utilitist grounds alone, is rightly considered one of the most rigid and inflexible of all the rules of morality. The exceptions to it should be rare and very narrowly defined. But nearly every moralist but Kant has admitted that there are such exceptions. What these are, and how the rules should be drawn that govern the exceptions, does not need to be considered in detail here. We need merely take note that the rules of morality, and the rules of good manners, can and should be harmonized with each other.

No one in modern times has more clearly recognized the importance of manners than Edmund Burke:

"Manners are of more importance than laws. Upon them, in great measure, the laws depend. The law touches us but here and there, and now and then. Manners are what vex or soothe, corrupt or purify, exalt or debase, barbarize or refine us, by a constant, steady, uniform, insensible operation, like that of the air we breathe in. They give their whole form and color to our lives. According to their quality, they aid morals, they supply them, or they totally destroy them."[2]

---

1. *The Wisdom of Confucius,* ed. Miles Menander Dawson (Boston: International Pocket Library, 1932), pp. 57–58. See also *The Ethics of Confucius* by the same author (Putnam's).

2. Edmund Burke, *Letters on a Regicide Peace,* I, 1796.

CHAPTER 9

The Problem of Self-Sacrifice

1. "Individual" and "Society"

We have seen that there tends to be a *coincidence* between the actions or rules of action that best promote the interests of the individual in the long run and the rules of action that best promote the interests of society as a whole in the long run. We have seen that this coincidence tends to be greater the longer the period we take into consideration.

There is another consideration, which needs to be reemphasized. The *antithesis* so often drawn between the "individual" and "society" is false. Society is merely the name we give to the collection of individuals and their interrelations. It would be clarifying and useful, in fact, if in sociological, economic, and ethical discussion we were most commonly to define society as *other people*. Then, in a society consisting only of three persons—A, B, and C—A, from his own point of view, is "the Individual," and B and C are "Society," whereas B, from his own point of view, is "the Individual" and A and C, "Society," etc.[1]

Now each of us *sees* himself sometimes as the individual and sometimes as a member of society. In the former role he is apt to emphasize the necessity of liberty and in the latter the necessity of law and order. A as a member of society is concerned that neither B nor C do anything to injure him. He insists that laws be passed to prevent this; and injuries that cannot satisfactorily be prevented by law he seeks to prevent by condemnation or disapproval. But he soon realizes that he cannot consistently or successfully use devices of condemnation or praise to influence the actions of others without accepting them for like actions by himself. Both to seem consistent to others and

65

to be consistent in his own eyes (for the "rational" man tends to accept consistency as an end in itself) he feels an obligation to accept for himself the moral rules he seeks to impose on others. (This is part of the explanation of the origin and growth of conscience.)

And the moral rules that we seek, for egoistic reasons, to impose on others, do not stop at inducing them not to inflict positive injury on us. If we found ourselves on board a ship sinking at sea we would think it the moral duty of those on any vessels nearby to answer our SOS signals, and to come to our rescue, even at considerable risk to themselves.

I do not mean to imply by this that all moral rules arise out of egoistic considerations. There are people who are spontaneously so moved by the suffering of others or a danger to others that they do not need to imagine themselves in the same predicament in order to think it their duty to come to the rescue of others. They will do so out of their spontaneous desire. Nearly all of us, in fact, do take spontaneous satisfaction in the happiness of others—at least of *some* others. What I am concerned to point out is that even if we were to assume, with Hobbes, that people are guided only by egoistic motives, we would probably arrive at the conclusion that they would be driven, in the end, to impose virtually the same outward code of morals on each other as if they were guided by altruistic motives as well. And because it is to the interest of each individual to live in a society characterized not only by peace and order and justice, but by social cooperation and mutual affection and aid, it is in the interest of each individual himself to help to create or preserve such a society through his own code and his own example.

We must repeat once more, then, that the *antithesis* between the interests of the Individual and the interests of Society is false. *Normally* and *usually* the actions that best promote the happiness and well-being of the individual best promote the happiness and well-being of the whole society. There is normally, to repeat, a *coincidence* between the long-run interests of the individual and the long-run interests of society. But we must frankly face the fact that there is not a complete *identity*. There will be times when the interests of the individual, even his interests in the long run, appear in his own eyes to conflict with those of society. What, then, is his duty? By what rule should he be guided? What should the moral code prescribe?

In examining this conflict, or apparent conflict, it will be profitable to move from the easier to the harder examples. What appears easiest at first glance is the establishment of a negative rule. Adam Smith states such a rule in sweeping form: "One individual must never prefer himself so much even to any other individual as to hurt or injure that other in order to benefit himself, though the benefit to the one should be much greater than the hurt or injury to the other. The poor man must neither defraud nor steal from the rich, though the acquisition might be much more beneficial to the one than the loss could be hurtful to the other."[2]

Here the specific illustration is beyond dispute, but the statement of the principle is much less so. The reason stealing is wrong under any conditions, as Adam Smith later points out, is that it is a violation of "one of those sacred rules upon the tolerable observation of which depend the whole security and peace of human society."[3]

2. Duty vs. Risk

But surely it cannot be wrong to do *anything* to benefit oneself simply because an incidental consequence may be to hurt or injure the interests of another. Should one reject the offer of a better job than one already has, simply because the present occupant, or another candidate, may then lose that particular job and may not be able to get another as good? Should a scientist refuse to publish a truthful criticism of another scientist's work because the result of that criticism may be to increase the first scientist's reputation at the cost of destroying the reputation of the scientist criticized? Evidently the rule proposed by Adam Smith would have to be carefully qualified to forbid injury to others only through coercion, violence, malice, misrepresentation, or fraud—i.e., the class of actions forbidden must be only those that tend to injure the long-run interests of society as a whole, and the class of actions prescribed must be only those that tend to benefit the long-run interests of society as a whole.

Turning to positive rules—i.e., those that enjoin help rather than those which merely forbid injury—let us begin with the athletic young man with a rope and a life-belt at hand (previously referred to on p. 51, who sits on a bench in a park along a river bank, and quietly sees a child drown, although he could rescue the child without the least danger. There can be no moral defense for such inaction. As Bentham pointed out, not only should it "be made the duty of every man to save another from mischief, when it can be done without prejudicing himself," but it might well be made a duty legally enforceable upon him by punishment for nonfeasance.[4]

But what should be the rule when the risk to the would-be rescuer rises? Here the problem becomes difficult, and the answer may depend not only on the degree of the risk, but on the relationship (whether, e.g., that of parent or of stranger) of the potential rescuer to the person or persons to be rescued. (It may also depend on a numerical relation. For example, whether the situation is [1] one in which one person, say a sapper, or soldier whose job it is to get rid of enemy mines, may be asked to risk his life to save a hundred or a thousand, or [2] one in which a hundred or a thousand may be asked to risk their lives to save only one, say a king or a president who is being held as a hostage.)

The ethical problem here may be difficult to answer precisely because, for example, the degree of risk being run may be indeterminable unless the risk is actually undertaken. Many a man has been tortured by conscience all the rest of his life because he has suspected that cowardice or selfishness led him to overestimate a risk that he refused to take to save another.

If we turn for help to the answers given by traditional ethical systems and by "common sense" ethics we find them to be in some cases not only clear but stern. There are conditions under which these traditional codes demand not only that a man risk his life for others but that he be willing, indeed, to sacrifice it. A soldier who deserts or runs away in battle, a captain who violates the rule that he should be the last to leave his ship, a doctor who refuses to enter a city where there is an epidemic or to attend a patient suffering from a contagious disease, a fireman (or father) who fails to try to rescue a child or an invalid from a fire, an armed policeman who stands idly by or runs away when an innocent citizen is being held up by a bandit at the point of a gun—all these are condemned by nearly every traditional or common sense moral code.

And the reason for this condemnation is plain. A nation that cannot depend on the bravery and self-sacrifice of its armed forces is doomed to conquest or annihilation. The inhabitants of a city who could not depend on the willingness of their policemen to take risks would be overrun by criminals, and would not be safe in the streets. The welfare and survival of a whole community, in brief, may depend upon the willingness of certain individuals or groups to sacrifice themselves for the rest.

But the duty is not always clear. If an unarmed citizen happens to be near when another unarmed citizen is being held up at gunpoint, is it the duty of the former to try to take the gun away? If even a hundred other unarmed citizens are by when a bandit is robbing one of them at gunpoint, is it the duty of one of the bystanders to try to take the gun away? And which one? No doubt collectively they could succeed; but it is the first to try who takes the greatest risk.

The answer of common sense ethics to this situation is far from clear. The people who read in the next day's newspapers about a thug shooting a victim and getting away because a crowd of a hundred did nothing to stop him, may be righteously indignant, and contemptuous of those who were too cowardly to act. Some of those who were in the crowd will feel secretly ashamed of their inac-

tion, or at least a little uneasy. But most of them will argue to themselves or others that it would have been an act of sheer foolhardiness
for them to take the initiative in interfering.

3. Search for a General Rule

Can we find the answer to the problem of self-sacrifice in any
general rule or principle?

I think we can reject without any further argument the contention of a few contemporary ethical writers that it is *never* the
duty of an individual to sacrifice himself for others, or that it is even
"immoral" for him to do so. The examples we have cited, and the
reasons why such self-sacrifice may sometimes be necessary, are sufficient and clear.

On the other hand, we do not need to give prolonged examination to the precisely opposite extreme contention that self-sacrifice
is the *normal* ethical requirement and that we need not count its
cost. Both Bentham in "The Constitutional Code" (*Works*, 1843)
and Spencer (*Data of Ethics,* 1901) have shown the folly of everybody's living and sacrificing for everybody else. Spencer proved by
specific arguments that a *misconceived* or *short-sighted* pursuit of
self-interest is not really in one's self-interest, and that a *misconceived* or *short-sighted* benevolence or self-sacrifice for the imagined
good of others is not really beneficent, and harms, rather than promotes the long-run good of others or the ultimate well-being of
society. These arguments are accepted by most modern ethical writers. "A society in which everybody spent his life sacrificing all his
pleasure for others would be even more absurd than a society whose
members all lived by taking in each other's washing. In a society of
such completely unselfish people who would be prepared to accept
and benefit by the sacrifice?[5]

Nevertheless the doctrine of sacrifice for sacrifice's sake was not
only held by Kant and other eminent moral philosophers, but is still
found in more modern writers. "Were there no use possibly to be

made of it, no happiness which could possibly be promoted, generous and self-forgetting action would be worth having in the universe."[6] This is sanctifying a means while ignoring its purpose. As E. F. Carritt rightly replies: "One can not act generously if one can find nothing that anybody wants, and self-forgetfulness, when there was nothing else practicable to remember, would be simply self-neglecting."[7]

With these two extremes out of the way, we can try to formulate an acceptable rule. Suppose we frame and examine the rule as follows:

Self-sacrifice is only required or justified where it is necessary in order to secure for another or others a greater good than that sacrificed.[8]

This is substantially the rule proposed by Jeremy Bentham—except that he would have used the word "pleasure" or "happiness" rather than "good." It is the rule of all the moral philosophers who have argued, with Adam Smith, that it is the duty of the agent to act in the way that an "impartial spectator" would approve.[9] "The point is that the interests of others should be treated on just the same level as one's own, so that the antithesis between self and others is made as little prominent in one's ethical thinking as possible."[10]

Now it is at least reasonably clear that no one should sacrifice his own interests to another or others unless a *greater* good is accomplished by the sacrifice than is lost to the agent. This is clear even from the most impartial view. Any rule of action should tend to promote a net gain of good on the whole rather than a net loss.

4. The Concept of Costs

Here we may draw a parallel not only with what has already been said about the requirements of simple prudence, but with the whole conception of *costs* in human action. The only rational prudential reason why a man should give up a pleasure, a satisfaction, or a good is to gain a greater pleasure, satisfaction, or good. This greater good may, of course, be nothing more than the absence of the subsequent pain or suffering caused by excessive indulgence in the pleasure given up—as a man may give up excessive drinking or smoking or eating in order to feel better in the long run—to improve his health and prolong his life. Prudential sacrifices are usually sacrifices of immediate pleasures or satisfactions in order to enjoy greater future happiness or satisfactions.

This is merely an illustration in the moral field of a "law of costs" that is usually discussed only in economic textbooks, but which in fact covers the whole realm of human action. "Everything, in short, is produced at the expense of foregoing something else. Costs of production themselves, in fact, might be defined as the things that are given up (the leisure and pleasures, the raw materials with alternative potential uses) in order to create the thing that is made."[11]

Costs thus conceived in "real" terms are sometimes distinguished by economists from money costs by the special name *opportunity costs*. This means, as the name implies, that we can do one thing only at the expense of foregoing something else. We can seize one opportunity only at the cost of foregoing what we consider the next best opportunity. Mises defines the concept in its broadest form:

> Action is an attempt to substitute a more satisfactory state of affairs for a less satisfactory one. . . . What gratifies less is abandoned in order to attain something that pleases more. That which is abandoned is called the price paid for the attainment of the end sought. The value of the price paid is called costs. Costs are equal to the value attached to the satisfaction which one must forego in order to attain the end aimed at.[12]

Or, more precisely and technically: "Costs are the value attached to the most valuable want-satisfaction which remains unsatisfied because the means required for its satisfaction are employed for that want-satisfaction the cost of which we are dealing with."[13]

This concept, unfortunately, is not very commonly understood or applied by writers on ethics. When we do apply it to the moral field, it is clear that every action we take must involve a *choice* of one value at the *expense* of other values. We cannot realize all values at once. We cannot realize more of one value without realizing less of another. We cannot give more time to learning one subject, or developing one skill, for example, without giving less time to learning some other subject or developing some other skill. We cannot achieve more of one good without achieving less of some other good. All good, all value, can be achieved only at the cost of foregoing some lesser good or value.

In brief, a "sacrifice," in the sense of a cost, is inescapable in all moral action as it is in all (narrowly conceived) "economic" action. In economics, the excess of the value gained over the value sacrificed is called a "profit." Because of the pejorative sense in which this word is commonly used by socialists and others, some readers may be shocked by its application to the realm of morality. But it is merely another way of saying that what is gained by an action should be greater than what is lost by it. In the broadest sense, "profit is the difference between the higher value of the good obtained and the lower value of the good sacrificed for its obtainment."[14]

This higher net value gained is of course the test of decisions and actions that concern oneself alone. It is the justification of the prudential virtues. But it should also be the test of actions that affect others. A man's duty cannot require that he give up any good of his own except for the *greater* good of another or others. In fact, it can reasonably be argued that it would be *immoral* for him to go beyond this—to sacrifice his own good to confer a *lesser* good on others. For the net effect of this would be to *reduce* the amount of good, to reduce the amount of happiness and well-being, in the universe.

I consider self-sacrifice essentially a *means*—a means sometimes necessary for promoting the end of maximum happiness and well-being for the whole community. But its value is wholly *instrumental* or *derivative* (like the value, in economic life, of irksome labor, or a raw material or a capital good). To the extent that an overzealous or misdirected self-sacrifice tends to *reduce* the sum of human happiness and well-being, its value is lost or becomes negative. It is therefore a mere confusion of thought to consider Self-Sacrifice (or Duty or Virtue) an *additional* good or value independent of the ultimate purpose it serves.

What leads to the confusion is the difficulty, if not the impossibility, of conceiving of a society in which happiness and well-being were maximized but in which nobody ever sacrificed his short-run interests to the long-run interests of others, in which nobody ever did his duty, and in which nobody had any virtues. But the reason for the difficulty or impossibility of conceiving such a society is that it involves a self-contradiction in concept and in terms. For the same reason it would be an impossibility to conceive of an economic community in which the production of ultimate consumer goods and services was maximized without the use of labor, raw materials, factories, machines, or means of transport. What we *mean* by rational Self-Sacrifice and Duty and Virtue is performing acts that tend to promote the maximum of happiness and well-being for the whole community and refraining from acts that tend to reduce such happiness and well-being. If the effect of Self-Sacrifice were to *reduce* the sum of happiness and well-being it would not be rational to admire it, and if the effect of other alleged duties and virtues were to *reduce* the sum of human happiness and well-being, we would cease to call them duties and virtues.

5. Obligations Have Limits

Let us return, then, to the word Self-Sacrifice and to the rule which we framed on page 71 that self-sacrifice is only required or justified where it is necessary in order to secure for another or others a *greater* good than that sacrificed. This rule sets an upper limit on altruism or self-sacrifice. But may not even this often set the upper limit too high? Does it not in fact ignore the highly personal and *circumstantial* nature of our duty? Other people do not stand to me merely in the relation of fellow human beings. They may also stand to me in the relation of promiser to promisee, of creditor to debtor, of employer to employee, of doctor to patient, of client to attorney, of wife to husband, of child to parent, of friend to friend, of business colleague or of fellow countryman. As Sir David Ross points out, each of these relations may be the foundation of a *prima facie* duty, which is more or less incumbent on me according to the circumstances of the case.[15] Can the abstract rule be extended indefinitely to cover all mankind, all strangers, no matter where in the world they may be found?

Americans are not only being importuned by private charities, but compulsorily taxed by their own government, to give food and aid and dollars to millions all over the world whom they will never see. What is their real obligation in this field? And when can they consider it discharged?

Suppose we conclude that sacrifice is required whenever it will yield more happiness to those for whom it is made than it will cost in happiness to those who make the sacrifice? It could plausibly be argued that, when we give this an objective or material interpretation, it would require us to keep giving away our fortunes or income or food as long as we had any more of any of these than the most miserably housed or clothed or fed person alive. We should have to keep giving, in other words, down to the point of absolute world equality of income and living standards.

Such an equal distribution of income, housing, clothing, and food, quantitatively and qualitatively, would be, of course not only physically impossible, but inconceivable. The attempt to achieve it, even by "voluntary" means and through pure moral approval and disapproval, would so tremendously reduce the incentives to work and production at both ends of the economic scale as to lead toward universal impoverishment. It would enormously reduce, and not increase, the sum of human happiness and well-being. The attempt to achieve such an egalitarian altruism, the attempt to impose such practically limitless and bottomless responsibilities, would bring misery and tragedy to mankind far beyond any harm resulting from the most complete "selfishness." (In fact, as Joseph Butler pointed out, and as many have recognized since, if everyone were constantly guided by a rational, enlightened, and far-sighted "egoism," the world would be an immensely better place than it is.)[16] But, some readers may say, I have been presenting an argument that does not really touch the rule we have been testing. By hypothesis, the sacrifices we are enjoined to make are only those that will yield *more* happiness in the long run to those for whom they are made than they will cost in *less* happiness (in the long run) to those who make them. Therefore we are asked to make *only* such sacrifices as will tend in the long run to *increase* the sum of happiness.

This is true. But even if we bypass here the crucial question whether it is possible to speak validly of a *sum* of happiness, or possible to compare the "increase" of one man's happiness with the "decrease" of another's, the preceding discussion will also show that it is very dangerous to give this principle any merely physical or short-term interpretation—or to base our duty, say, on any mathematical income comparisons. The less our active sympathies with the persons we are called upon to help, the more remote such persons are from our direct acquaintance and daily lives, the more reluctant we will be to make any sacrifice to help them, the less satisfaction we will take in any sacrifice—and, conversely, the less likely are those helped to appreciate the sacrifice on our part or to be permanently benefited by it.

The ethical problem here is complicated by the fact that certain acts of so-called "sacrifice" are not considered by those who make them to be sacrifices at all. Such are the sacrifices that a mother makes for her child. Certainly as long as the child is very young and truly helpless, most such sacrifices may directly and immediately, as well as in the long run, increase the happiness both of the one who makes the "sacrifice" and the one for whom it is made. Such sacrifices present an ethical problem of limitation only when they are carried to the point where they may either permanently impair the ability of the benefactor to continue his or her sacrifices or where they coddle or spoil or in some other way demoralize the child or other intended beneficiary.

6. Maxima and Minima

But the problem we are concerned with here is whether it is possible to frame a *general rule* to apply to the duty or limits of self-sacrifice—for the benefit of people, say, whom we may not know, or even for the benefit of people whom we may not like. One difficulty of such a general rule is that it cannot be simple. Our duty or non-duty may depend upon the relations, as I have previously hinted, in which we find ourselves with other people, relations which may sometimes be accidental. Thus if we are walking along a lonely road, even if we are on a temporary visit to a foreign country, and find a man who has been seriously injured by an automobile, or robbed, beaten, and left half dead, we cannot pass by "on the other side" and tell ourselves that the whole matter is none of our business, and besides we are late for an appointment. Our duty is to act as the Good Samaritan did. But this does not mean that our duty is to take all the world's burdens on our own shoulders, or to keep constantly touring around trying to find people to save, regardless of how they got into their predicament or what the long-run effect of our rescue operations would be on them.

This means that we must carefully distinguish between the special case and the general rule, or even between any single instance considered in isolation and a general rule. If you give a dollar to a beggar, or even $1,000 to a chance pauper who "needs" the money more than you do, a mathematical comparison of the supposed marginal utility of the money to him with its supposed much smaller marginal utility to you (assuming such a comparison were possible) may seem to result in a net gain of happiness for the two of you considered together. But to erect this into a general rule, to impose it as a general obligation, would result in a net loss of happiness for the community considered as a whole.

In brief, a single act of indiscriminate charity (or discriminate only in the sense of moving toward equalization of income without any other criterion) may seem to increase the happiness of the recipient more than it reduces the happiness of the donor. But if such extensive and practically limitless charity were erected into a *general moral rule* imposed on us it would lead to a great diminution of happiness because it would encourage permanent mendicancy in increasing numbers of people, who would come to regard such help as a "right," and would tend to discourage effort and industry on the part of those on whom this moral burden was imposed.

Let us now try to sum up the drift of our discussion. It may often be extremely difficult in practice to know how to apply our principle that self-sacrifice is occasionally necessary, though only when it seems likely to result in an increase in the sum of happiness and well-being. Limitless charity, or a limitless *obligation* to charity, is unlikely to achieve this result. All of us cannot sell all that we have, and give it to the poor.[17] Universalized, the idea becomes self-contradictory: there would be no one to sell to. Between never doing a charitable act, and giving away one's all, lies a wide range of possibilities for which no definite and clean-cut rule can be laid down. It may be right to contribute to a certain cause but not wrong not to.

But if the problem cannot be solved with precision, it does not follow that it cannot be solved at least within certain upper and lower limits. The upper limit, as we have seen, is that no act of self-sacrifice is justified unless it secures for another a *greater* good than the good that is sacrificed. The lower limit is, of course, that one should refrain from any positive harm to one's neighbors. In between is a twilight zone of obligation.

The problem can probably be solved within closer maxima and minima than this.[18] The overriding guide to rules of ethics is social cooperation. The rules we should establish for mutual obligation are those that, when generalized, tend most to promote social cooperation.

Moral rules are designed precisely to promote individual interest to the maximum extent. The true contrast is between the kind of self-interest that is incompatible with the interest of others and the kind of self-interest that is compatible with the interest of others. Just as the best traffic rules are those that promote the maximum flow of safe traffic for the most cars, so the best moral rules are those that promote the maximum self-interest for the most people. It would be a contradiction in terms to say that the maximum interest of all was promoted by everyone's *restricting* the pursuit of his own interest. True, *some* must forego the pursuit of certain *apparent* or *temporary* advantages because these are of the kind that would thwart the achievement of the real interests not only of most others but even of himself. But the happiness of *all* cannot be maximized unless the happiness of *each* is maximized.

If we have a society consisting (let us say for simplicity) of only two people, A and B, then the rules of conduct they should adopt and adhere to are not those that are solely in A's interest, nor solely in B's interest, but most in the long-run interest of *both*. The rules that are most in the interest of *both* must be in the long run the rules that are most in the interest of *each*. This remains true when our hypothetical society is increased from A and B to everybody from A to Z.

This *mutualism* is the reconciliation of "self-interest" and "morality." For one best promotes one's own interest in the long run precisely by abiding by the rules that best promote the interest of *everyone,* and by cooperating with others to hold everyone *else* to those rules. If it is to *everyone's* long-run interest to adhere to and uphold the moral rules, it must therefore be to *mine*.

To sum up: The ideal moral rules are those that are most con-

ducive to social cooperation and therefore to the realization of the
greatest possible number of interests for the greatest possible number of people. The very function of morality, as Toulmin has put it,
is "to correlate our feelings and behavior in such a way as to make
the fulfilment of everyone's aims and desires as far as possible compatible."[19] But just as *all* interests, major and minor, long-term and
short- term, cannot be realized all the time (partly because some are
inherently unachievable and partly because some are incompatible
with others) so not *everybody's* interests can be realized all the time.
If we think of such a rare crisis example as people taking to the
lifeboats of a sinking ship, then an orderly and mutualistic procedure, as contrasted with a disorderly and sordid stampede, will maximize the number of people who can be saved. But even in the
"moral" procedure *some* people may have to be sacrificed. And
though they will be *fewer* people than would have been sacrificed in
an immoral scramble, they may none the less be *different* people. A
few of those who are lost *may* have been among those who could
have saved themselves by ruthlessness. The ideal moral rules, therefore, may not only sometimes oblige an individual to make some
immediate or temporary sacrifice in his own long-run interest, but
even (though very rarely) to sacrifice even his own long-run interest
to the larger long-run interest of everybody else.

We come back once more to the conclusion that the real interests of the individual and of society nearly always *coincide,* but are
not (such is our human predicament) in every case *identical.*

---

1. One of the most helpful methods of ethics (as it is of economics) is the use
of simplifying imaginary constructions, or "models." Problems of the relation of
the "individual" to "society" might in many cases be clarified by: (1) imagining the
necessary prudential ethics of a Crusoe on a desert island; (2) imagining the ideal
ethical relations (including the necessary extent of mutual cooperation and acceptance of mutual obligation) appropriate in an isolated society of two, in which for
each individual "society" is merely *the other person;* and (3) finally, imagining the
ethics most appropriate in a society of three or more.

2. Adam Smith, *The Theory of Moral Sentiments* (1759), Sect. III, Chap. III.

3. *Loc. cit.*

4. Jeremy Bentham, *Morals and Legislation*, p. 323.

5. A. C. Ewing, *Ethics* (New York: Macmillan, 1953), pp. 31–32.

6. J. Grote, *Treatise on the Moral Ideals*, Chap. VI, p. 76.

7. E. F. Carritt, *The Theory of Morals* (London: Oxford University Press, 1928), p. 54.

8. This is a paraphrase of a rule suggested (but suspected by him of being a little too exact and niggardly) by A. C. Ewing, *Ethics*, p. 32.

9. Adam Smith, *The Theory of Moral Sentiments*, Sec. III, Chap. III.

10. A. C. Ewing, *Ethics*, p. 33.

11. Henry Hazlitt, *Economics in One Lesson*, p. 114.

12. Ludwig von Mises, *Human Action*, p. 97.

13. *Ibid.*, p. 393.

14. Ludwig von Mises, *Theory and History*, p. 210.

15. David Ross, *The Right and the Good* (Oxford: Clarendon Press, 1930), p. 19.

16. Joseph Butler, *Fifteen Sermons* (1726). ["I must however remind you that though benevolence and self-love are different, though the former tends most directly to public good, and the latter to private, yet they are so perfectly coincident that the greatest satisfactions to ourselves depend upon our having benevolence in a due degree, and that self-love is one chief security of our right behavior toward society. It may be added that their mutual coinciding, so that we can scarce promote one without the other, is equally a proof that we were made for both." Quoted (pp. 98–100) in Hazlitt's *Foundations of Morality*, unabridged (1964/98).—Ed.]

17. Some theologians argue that Jesus did not intend this advice for everybody. It was given explicitly only to a rich young man who aspired to be one of his disciples: "If thou wilt be perfect, go and sell that thou hast, and give to the poor, and thou shalt have treasure in heaven" (Matthew 19:21). Other theologians, while arguing that such advice was intended for all of Christ's followers, contend that it was based on the assumption that "the Kingdom of God is at hand" (Mark 1:15), and not on the assumption of a permanent life for man in this world.

18. It seems probable that we would make greater progress in the social sciences generally (including political science, economic policy, and jurisprudence as well as ethics) if we abandoned the preconception that every problem could be solved with precision according to some single and simple abstract principle, and resigned ourselves to recognizing that some social problems can be solved only within a certain "twilight" *zone*, only within certain upper and lower limits, certain maxima and minima. This may apply to such problems as the proper sphere and limits of state power, levels and types of taxation, the laws governing libel, obscenity, boycotts, and picketing, as well as the extent and limits of mutual obligation, aid, or cooperation.

19. Stephen Toulmin, *An Examination of the Place of Reason in Ethics* (Cambridge: University Press, 1950), p. 137.

CHAPTER 10

Absolutism *vs.* Relativism

1. The Dilemma of Hume and Spencer

One of the central problems of ethics is the extent to which its rules and imperatives are absolute or merely relative. The chief reason why the problem still lacks a satisfactory solution is that its very existence is so seldom explicitly recognized. On the one hand are absolutists like Kant,* and his tacit assumption that our duties are always simple, clear, and never in conflict.[1] On the other hand are the ethical anarchists or *ad hoc* utilitarians who contend that general rules are unnecessary, impracticable, or absurd, and that every ethical decision must be based entirely on the particular circumstances of the moment and the specific "merits of the case." That our duties may be absolute in some respects, and relative in others, is a possibility that is too seldom considered—still less the problem of the precise limits of absolutism and relativism respectively.

One of the few moral philosophers who gave specific and extensive consideration to the problem is Herbert Spencer; and though his discussion is unsatisfactory in many respects, it states some important truths, and can still serve as a profitable starting point for consideration.

Spencer begins[2] by criticizing an early sentence (later apparently omitted) in the first edition of Henry Sidgwick's *Methods of Ethics:* "That there is in any given circumstances some one thing which ought to be done, and that this can be known, is a fundamental

---

*Ed. note, According to Immanual Kant, as quoted in the unabridged version of this book (p. 143) "There is therefore but one categorical imperative, namely this: Act only on that maxim whereby thou canst at the same time will that it should become a universal law."

assumption made not by philosophers only, but by all who perform any processes of moral reasoning." Spencer answers: "Instead of admitting that there is in every case a right and a wrong, it may be contended that in multitudinous cases no right, properly so called, can be alleged, but only a least wrong." And further, "in many of these cases . . . it is not possible to ascertain with any precision which is the least wrong."

He proceeds to give a number of illustrations. For example: "The transgressions or short-comings of a servant vary from the trivial to the grave, and the evils which discharge may bring range through countless degrees from slight to serious. The penalty may be inflicted for a very small offence, and then there is wrong done, or, after numerous grave offences, it may not be inflicted, and again there is wrong done. How shall be determined the degree of transgression beyond which to discharge is less wrong than not to discharge?"

He proceeds to other illustrations: Under what conditions is a merchant justified in borrowing to save himself from bankruptcy, when he is also risking the funds of the friend from whom he borrows? To what extent can a man neglect his duty to his family in fulfilling what appears to be a peremptory public duty?

The illustrations that Spencer gives of conflicting considerations and conflicting duties are all real and all valid, though perhaps comparatively trivial. This conflict may exist in the most crucial human decisions. War is a dreadful recourse. It has usually brought far greater evils in its train than those that provoked the resort to war even by those originally on the "defensive." Does this mean that no nation should ever resort to war under any provocation whatever—that it should submit to dishonor, humiliation, tribute, subservience, invasion, servility, enslavement, even annihilation? Is there any wisdom in propitiation, nonresistance, appeasement? Or does this only encourage the aggressor? At just what point is resort to war justifiable? The same questions may be asked in regard to submitting to despotism and deprivation of property or liberty, or

starting a revolt or revolution of uncertain outcome or consequence. Here indeed we are confronted by choices in which there is
no absolutely right but only a relatively right decision—in which, in
fact, there may seem to be no solution at all that is "right" but only
one that is least wrong.

Then Spencer turns to another but similar problem. He argues
that the coexistence of a perfect man and an imperfect society is
impossible:

> . . . [I]deal conduct such as ethical theory is concerned
> with, is not possible for the ideal man in the midst of men
> otherwise constituted. An absolutely just or perfectly sym-
> pathetic person could not live and act according to his
> nature in a tribe of cannibals. Among people who are
> treacherous and utterly without scruple, entire truthfulness
> and openness must bring ruin. If all around recognize only
> the law of the strongest; one whose nature will not allow
> him to inflict pain on others must go to the wall. There
> requires a certain congruity between the conduct of each
> member of a society and others' conduct. A mode of action
> entirely alien to the prevailing modes of action cannot be
> successfully persisted in—must eventuate in death of self, or
> posterity, or both.

Spencer, of course, was not the first to pose this problem. It had
been raised more than a century before, with even greater force, by
David Hume:

> Suppose, likewise, that it should be a virtuous man's fate
> to fall into the society of ruffians, remote from the protec-
> tion of laws and government, what conduct must he
> embrace in that melancholy situation? He sees such a des-
> perate rapaciousness prevail, such a disregard to equity,
> such contempt of order, such stupid blindness to future con-

sequences, as must immediately have the most tragical conclusion and must terminate in destruction to the greater number and in a total dissolution of society to the rest. He, meanwhile, can have no other expedient than to arm himself, to whomever the sword he seizes, or the buckler, may belong; to make provision of all means of defense and security. And his particular regard to justice being no longer of use to his own safety or that of others, he must consult the dictates of self-preservation alone, without concern for those who no longer merit his care and attention.[3]

2. The Mirage of Perfection

Before examining some of the conclusions that Hume and Spencer respectively draw from this hypothetical situation, I should like to go on to examine some of the further and possibly even more basic difficulties in the conception of Absolute Ethics.

These difficulties, it seems to me, center around the concept of the Absolute and the concept of Perfection. I do not wish to get bogged down in the interminable discussions of the nature of the Absolute as found in metaphysical literature,[4] so I will confine myself to a discussion of the concept of Perfection.

Spencer, as we have seen, concludes that the "perfect man" can exist only in the "perfect society." If we carry his logic a step further, the perfect society can be conceived to exist only in a perfect world. Now to attempt to frame a conception of *perfection* seems to me to involve us in insoluble problems and contradictions. Let us begin with the concept of a perfect world.

A perfect world would be one in which all our desires were instantly and completely satisfied.[5] But in such a world desire itself could not come into existence. Desire is always a desire for change of some kind—for changing a less satisfactory state of affairs into a more satisfactory (or less unsatisfactory) one. The existence of a desire presupposes, in other words, that the existing state of affairs is not completely satisfactory. All thinking is primarily problem-solving. How could thinking exist with no problems to be solved? All activity or action is a striving for something, for a change or alteration in the existing state of affairs. Why should there be any striving, any action, when conditions are already perfect? Why should I sleep or waken, dress or undress, eat or diet, work or play, smoke or drink or abstain, think or talk or move, why should I raise my hand, or let it fall, why should I desire any action or change of any kind, when everything is perfect just as it is?

Our difficulties do not appreciably decrease when we try to imagine a perfect society or a perfect man in this perfect world. There would be no place for many of the ethical qualities that most moralists admire—effort, striving, persistence, self-denial, courage, and compassion. Those who believe that the great ethical goal of each of us should be to improve others, to incite them to more virtue, would find nothing to do. He who was already perfect would not have to struggle to improve or perfect himself.

"Self-perfection" is frequently laid down as a man's only true moral goal. But those who make it the goal dodge the difficulties by tacitly assuming that it is unattainable. They suggest that a man should strive to cultivate all his faculties, ignoring the fact that he can cultivate some only by relative neglect of others. By treating "self-perfection" as an end in itself, they avoid asking themselves what a man is going to do with his perfect character after he has achieved it. For the *perfectly* moral man not only must never do the slightest amount of harm but must always be doing positive good— otherwise he is less than perfect. He cannot make perfectly wise decisions unless he has infinite knowledge and clairvoyance, and can foresee all the consequences of his acts. The perfect man must exercise *unceasing* benevolence; but in a society of perfect men no one would have any opportunity or need to exercise benevolence.

In brief, it is the effort to conceive of an *absolute* ethics or a *perfect* world and society that has landed ethics, historically, into so much rhetoric and sterility. We are more likely to make sense by talking in the relative terms of *better* and *worse*. It is when we try to say what would be *worst* and what would be *best* that our difficulties mount. For to determine what is *best* is often to make a choice among an infinite number of possibilities. But if we ask, more modestly—What actions or rules of action would make things worse? What actions or rules of action would make things better?—we are often more likely to make progress. We would do well to dwell on the meaning and the important element of truth in Voltaire's aphorism: "The best is the enemy of the good."

But when we state the case against absolutism in ethics, we must be extremely careful not to overstate it, and so land in the bottomless swamp of relativism or moral anarchy.

Real ethical problems arise; real conflicts arise; but they are comparatively rare, and they are not insoluble. It is often difficult to say with confidence what is the best solution, but it is seldom difficult to say what is the worse and what is the *better* solution. Humanity has, over the generations, worked out moral traditions, rules, principles, which have survived, and are daily reinforced anew, precisely because they do solve the great majority of our moral problems, precisely because it has been found that, by adhering to them, we best achieve justice, social cooperation, and the long-run maximization of happiness or minimization of misery. We do not have to solve our daily moral problems, or make our daily moral decisions, by a fresh and special calculus of the probable total consequences of each act or decision over an infinity of time. The traditional moral rules save us from this. Only where they conflict, or are patently inadequate or inapplicable, are we thrown back on the necessity of thinking out our problem afresh, without any "guiding principle" or "method of estimation."

And even when we are thrown into the situation envisioned by Hume and Spencer we are not entirely without guiding principles. A completely moral man is not forced to be as savage and ruthless as the most savage and ruthless ruffian or scoundrel in the society, or even as savage and ruthless as the average. He is forced to defend himself and his family and his property; he must be constantly on guard against being robbed or swindled or betrayed; but he does not need himself to slaughter (except in self-defense) or rob or swindle or betray. His duty and salvation is to try to raise the average level of behavior both by setting an example and by letting others see that they do not need to fear him if they act decently.

The Hume-Spencer dilemma does show how tremendously threatening it is to individual ethics when the *general level* of ethics in a community deteriorates. The ethical standards and practices of the individual and the prevailing ethical standards and practices of the whole community are clearly *interdependent*. But if the ethical standards of the community help to determine the ethical standard of the individual, so do those of the individual help to determine those of the community. Criminals and scoundrels everywhere, invariably use as an excuse to themselves and others, that "everybody" does the crimes that they do, or "would if they had the nerve." In order to assure themselves that they are no worse than anybody else, they contend that nobody else is any better than they are. But the moral man, the man of honor, will never be satisfied to tell himself that he is as good as the average. He will recognize that his own long-run happiness, and the long-run happiness of the community, can only be furthered by raising the average. And this he will tend to do by his own example.

In fact, even in a "completely" demoralized community, the fear by each individual of assaults, depredations, and betrayals by others will incite individual and, finally, general efforts to restore peace and order and morality and mutual trust. Hence, when the moral "equilibrium" has been violently upset, the general unacceptability or intolerableness of the resulting situation may itself finally set in motion forces tending to restore the equilibrium. Yet irreparable harm may be done before this restoration can be brought about.

The morality of each is enormously influenced by the morality of all, and the morality of all by the morality of each. When everyone is moral, it is much easier for me to be so, and the pressure on me to be so (through the approval and disapproval of others) is also greater. But where everyone else is immoral I must fight, cheat, lie, betray, to survive—or at least I may tell myself that I must. And though self-corrective forces will doubtless finally set in, the misfortune is that an immoral social environment will probably incite immorality in the individual quicker than a moral social environment will encourage morality in him. That is why the general level of morality is never completely secure, and can be raised or even maintained only by the constant vigilance and effort of each of us.

3. Obligatory and Optional Ethics

So far in our discussion of absolute and relative ethics I have been using these terms in a different sense than that found in most contemporary discussion. Ethical "relativism" is frequently defined as meaning that morality is wholly relative to a particular place, time, or person. Sometimes it is used as a name for the doctrine that conflicting ethical opinions can be equally valid. We must reject relativism in either of these senses. There are basic moral principles that are valid for all ages and all peoples, for the simple reason that without them social life would be impossible.

This need not mean, however, that we must all be ethical absolutists in the rigid sense, say, that Kant was. Morality is primarily a means rather than an end in itself. It exists to serve human needs—which means the needs of man as he is or can become. A society of angels would not need a moral code. We should distinguish, therefore, between a minimum acceptable ethics, to which we can insist that everybody conform, and an ethics of supererogation—conduct which we do not expect of each other, but which we applaud and marvel at when it occurs.

The general moral code, in brief, should not impose excessive positive duties on us, so that we cannot even play, enjoy ourselves, or relax without a guilty conscience. Unless the code prescribes a level of conduct that most of us can reasonably hope to achieve, it will simply be disregarded. There must be definite limits to our duties. People must be allowed a moral breathing spell once in a while. The greatest happiness is promoted by rules that do not make the requirements of morality ubiquitous and oppressive. That is one reason why the negative Golden Rule: "Do not do unto others as you would not want others to do unto you" is a better rule of thumb, in most circumstances, than the positive Golden Rule.

---

1. Immanuel Kant, *Critique of Practical Reason, and Other Works on the Theory of Ethics,* trans. by T. K. Abbott, 6th ed. (Longmans, Green, 1909). Book II, Chapter II, p. 209.

2. All the subsequent quotations are from the chapter "Absolute and Relative Ethics" in Herbert Spencer's *Data of Ethics* (New York: P. F. Collier, 1901).

3. David Hume, *An Inquiry Concerning the Principles of Morals,* p. 18.

4. *E.g.,* F. H. Bradley, *Appearance and Reality* (London: Oxford, 1930).

5. A friendly critic has objected that this cannot apply to *all* our desires but only to all our *good* desires—for half the people, for instance, might desire the annihilation of all the rest. I think the suggested amendment superfluous, however; first, because a perfect world would be occupied only by perfect people, who would by definition have only good desires; and secondly, because *all* our desires could not be satisfied unless they were *all* compatible with each other.

CHAPTER 11

Vocation and Circumstance

1. Duties—Universal or Special?

Just as, in our economic life, there is a necessary division and specialization of labor, so in our moral life there is a necessary division and specialization of duty. Failure to recognize this has led to a great deal of confusion in ethical thought. It is commonly assumed that what is a duty for one must be a duty for all, and that what is not a duty for most of us cannot be made a duty for anyone. It is commonly assumed, in other words, that a duty must either be universal or it is not a duty at all. This is the common interpretation of Kant's rule: "Make the maxim of thy action that which thou wouldst at the same time to be universal law."

A little reflection will show, however, that each of us has special moral duties just as each of us has a special vocation and a special job. In fact, a large number of these special duties grow directly out of our special vocation and our special job. Just as it is the moral duty of each of us to fulfill the conditions of an economic contract, so it is the moral duty of each of us to fulfill the implied duties of any job we have accepted. And often, precisely because we have accepted these special duties, they are not the necessary duties of others.

Let us illustrate this by a few special situations. If you are walking alone along a deserted beach, and someone in the water is drowning and cries for help, and the distance from the shore, the waves and tide, your own swimming ability and other conditions are such that you can probably save him without excessive risk to your own life, then it is your duty to try.

But suppose, now, under the same conditions, a hundred people are on that beach? Your duty to undertake the rescue does not altogether disappear—*somebody* must be the rescuer— but it is considerably attenuated. The duty is heavier on the stronger swimmers than on the weaker ones—because their chances for success are higher and their risks to themselves are lower. And if there is on the beach a professional lifesaver specifically employed to watch that beach, then the duty is clearly his. If the lifeguard were absent, or ill, or drunk, or had just announced that he had gone on strike, then it would become the duty of someone else on the beach to undertake the rescue—but neither the law nor the rules of morality could say specifically *whose* duty. All one is entitled to say is that if no one at all undertook the rescue, and the victim drowned, everyone on that beach *capable* of having made the rescue would share the guilt of nonfeasance and would have good reason to feel ashamed of himself.

Clear specific vocation and specific assignment of duties solves many a moral problem of this sort. If you know that a helpless little girl or a woman invalid is in a burning building, is it your duty to try to save her? The answer depends on many circumstances—on the possibility of a successful attempt or the apparent hopelessness of it; on your particular relationship to the victim; on whether other possible rescuers, better-equipped, are present. But if professional firemen have arrived, with proper equipment, then the question whose duty it is—if the rescue is feasible at all—is practically settled.

Suppose a bandit on the street is holding someone up at the point of a gun. You happen to be there and are unarmed. Is it your duty to try to stop him, in spite of the huge risk? Suppose he starts to beat the victim with the butt of his gun? Does your duty to intervene become stronger? Or suppose—a situation that sometimes occurs—an armed bandit is robbing or shooting someone and a crowd of people are present? It is, most people would say, the crowd's duty to stop him. But one essential part of the question is usually left unanswered. Whose duty is it to make the first move— to try to take the gun away from the bandit?

Again, the answer to these questions must depend to some

extent on special circumstance—for instance, on whether the object of the bandit's attack is your wife, say, or a stranger. But one circumstance would definitely settle the question, in most people's opinion. If an armed policeman were on the scene, it would be *his* duty to take the risks of intervention.

Thus certain duties become clear and unequivocal for the simple reason that they have already been accepted either explicitly or implicitly by the adoption of a vocation or the acceptance of a particular job or assignment. We often speak of the "duties" of a particular job when referring merely to the routine requirements of it. But whenever failure to perform these requirements would do appreciable harm, these are moral duties also. No man who has no intention of assuming the risks necessary to the vocation he has voluntarily chosen—whether that of a policeman, soldier, ship captain, airplane pilot, fireman, lifeguard, night watchman, or doctor—has any right to adopt such a vocation.

"Common-sense" ethics suggests, as we have seen in the course of this discussion, that we have certain duties which might almost be called *duties of accident.* If we happen to be the only person on a beach when someone calls for help in the water, if we are in the first car to arrive when someone has met an accident or some pedestrian lies groaning on the road, we cannot tell ourselves that it is a mere accident that we, and we alone, happen to be at this precise spot at this precise moment, that rescue or help by us would be inconvenient, that we are somewhat in a hurry, that this is none of our business, and that someone else will probably be along a little later. A duty has fallen upon us—by accident, it is true—but it is none the less a duty. So of the three people who came upon the man who went down from Jerusalem to Jericho, and fell among thieves, the two who passed by on the other side were ignoring the plainest duty of compassion, and only the Good Samaritan was acting morally (Luke 10:30–33).

The rationale of this duty is clear enough. Any one of us would expect this of a passer-by if we were the man who had been beaten and robbed. And a world in which passers-by did not accept such a duty is one that no one could envisage as a truly moral world.

2. The Limits of Responsibility

Yet we would greatly underrate the importance of such duties if we called them "duties of accident." A much better term would be *duties of circumstance* or *duties of relation.* And the latter term would cover not only the duties that fall to us because of our *blood* relation to some other person or persons—the duties of consanguinity—but the duties that fall to us because of our relationships of all kinds, sometimes even spatial, to other persons—the duties of *proximity.*

None of us is an abstract or disembodied spirit. Each of us is a citizen of a particular country, a resident of a particular city or a particular neighborhood, a son or daughter, a father or mother, a brother or sister, a husband or wife, a friend or acquaintance, an employer or employee, a business colleague, or fellow worker, a neighbor, a tradesman or his customer, a doctor or his patient, a lawyer or his client, or, temporarily, a fellow traveler with others in the same boat or the same bus. And in each of these capacities he has assumed certain explicit or implied duties to other specific persons. It is a man's duty to support and defend his own wife but not necessarily anybody else's. It is a man's duty to provide for the education of his own children but not necessarily for other people's children. If a man is driving his car along a lonely road and comes upon a motorist who has had a serious accident, it is his duty, even if he happens to be in a foreign country, or is on that road by the merest chance, to stop and do what he reasonably can to help.

But it is precisely because each of us has so many special duties of vocation, relation, or proximity that he cannot and does not have limitless duties in all directions. If we come upon someone in distress, and we are the only source of help available to him at the moment, it is our duty to do what we reasonably can to relieve him.

But it is not, therefore, our duty to go around *looking* for people to help. It is not our duty to meddle in other people's affairs or to force our assistance on them. In the world today, someone is dying with almost every tick of the clock. In the United States alone three people die every minute. Somewhere, we may be sure, perhaps in Korea or in Paraguay, some people must be suffering or starving. But it does not follow that it is our duty to drop whatever we are doing and help; or even to let ourselves be endlessly taxed for bottomless "foreign aid" distributed by well-paid bureaucrats who constantly search for possible aid-recipients and derive a sense of immense self-righteousness from their vicarious generosity. Nor does it follow that, because of our abstract knowledge of death and suffering *somewhere,* we must develop a guilt-complex because we happen at the moment to be enjoying ourselves.

The conclusion that each of us has special duties, in brief, peculiar to his vocation, relation, or circumstances, must have as its corollary and obverse the conclusion that the duty of each of us has certain definite limits.

3. "All Mankind"—Or Your Neighbor

Some utilitarians tell us that each of us, on the basis of the goal of maximizing human happiness, should be willing by a benevolent action to sacrifice his own happiness at least up to the point where his action reduces it less than it can increase the happiness of another. Common sense morality would reply, I think, that much depends on *what* the sacrifice is and on *who* this "other" is. If he or she is one's wife or daughter or other loved one, the rule seems acceptable enough: in such a case, in fact, it may be doubtful that one is really sacrificing any of his own happiness at all. But if the person for whom one is asked to make this sacrifice is a complete stranger, or someone that one knows but detests, I doubt that common sense morality would accept any such mathematical calculation for "maximizing human happiness," even if it were in fact possible to measure the decrease in one's own happiness against the increase of the stranger's.

Is it possible to solve this problem in abstract terms or by definite general rules? Let us at least try; and let us begin by looking at the implicit but rather nebulous rules that have been worked out by common sense morality, to see whether they can furnish us with any clue.

The spirit of that morality leads us to be properly suspicious, I think, of the modern reformer, typified by Rousseau or Marx, whose professed love for all mankind is so often accompanied by neglect of or callousness toward his own family and friends. "For the social courtesies and minor loyalties of life," once wrote Albert Jay Nock, "give me the old fogy every time in preference to radicals . . . or indeed most of us. We are so taken up with our general love for humanity that we don't have time to be decent to anybody."[1]

And perhaps this result is not accidental. I suspect that the classical utilitarians slipped into a confusion of thought, which can have, and has already had, some pernicious consequences. It is one thing, and correct, to say that our moral rules should be such as to promote the maximum happiness for all humanity. But it is a questionable corollary that it is, therefore, the duty of each individual himself to attempt to promote directly the maximum general happiness for all humanity. For the best way to promote this maximum general happiness may be for each individual to cooperate with, and perform his duties toward, his immediate family, neighbors, and associates.

I hope I may be forgiven if I attempt to clarify and illustrate the point by a graphic illustration. In the chart (Fig. 1) A has direct ties of family, friendship, business, or neighborhood with B, C, D, and E, and corresponding (reciprocal) obligations and duties. If A takes care of these, and B, C, D, and E respectively take care of *their* direct ties and duties, and so throughout, then *total* social cooperation and mutual helpfulness is assured. But if A is told or believes that he not only has direct duties toward B, C, D, and E, but *equal*

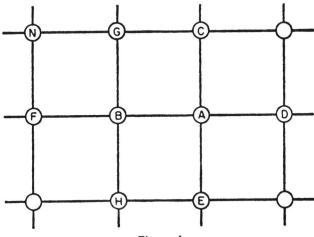

Figure 1

duties and obligations toward N, and toward a practically infinite number of N's, the sheer impossibility of fulfilling any such duties and obligations may cause him to slight or abandon his direct duties to those near him. If his duty to N, a stranger, is no less than that to B, his brother, he may unconsciously reason that then his duty to B is no greater than his duty to N—and he may therefore neglect both, or give them both mere lip-service. But if A fulfills his direct duties to B, etc., and B fulfills his direct duties to A, H, F, and G, then F and G can be depended on to cooperate with N, etc.

It may, perhaps, never be possible to reduce to any precise rule the strength and urgency of A's duty to B as compared with his remote and indirect duty to N, etc. Possibly one day some law may be formulated that is equivalent in the moral realm to the law of gravitation in the physical, according to which one's duties to others decrease, say, as the square of the "distance" increases (or increase inversely as the square of the "distance" decreases). Meanwhile, we can only be guided by the rather nebulous rules that have been worked out by common sense morality. But these nebulous rules do, I think, implicitly follow some such Principle of Proximity as the one I have here outlined—a duty of person-to-person rather than of person-to-people, of each-to-each rather than of each-to-all or each-to-humanity, which the classical utilitarians too hastily adopted. For there is much wisdom in the proverb: "What's everybody's business is nobody's business." And a corollary is: What's everybody's vague "responsibility" tends to be nobody's real responsibility.

But here we are brought to a major problem that has received astonishingly little discussion by moral philosophers. We have recognized validity in Kant's precept: "Act as if the law of thy action were to become by thy will law universal." Many have drawn from this the corollary that *all* moral rules should be "universalizable." But now we seem to be saying the opposite: that the duties of each of us are particular, depending upon our vocation, our "station," or our special relations with others.

Is there really a contradiction here? Or is there some way in which we can reconcile the necessary *universality* with the necessary *particularity* of duties? Such a reconciliation is possible, I think, if we state each person's duty correctly. Then we would say, for example, that every mother has duties toward her *own* children, every husband toward his *own* wife, every man toward his *own* job and his *own* employer, every employer toward his *own* employees, etc. Thus we can state the rule or the duty so that it is at once particular and of universal application.

Another way of reconciling the necessary universality with the necessary particularity of duties is to say that a man's duty depends *on the particular circumstances* in which he finds himself or in which he is asked to act; and that *his* duty in *those* circumstances would be *any*one's or *every*one's duty in the *same* circumstances. The difficulty with this solution is that no two people ever do find themselves in *exactly* the same circumstances, and that some circumstances are *morally relevant* and others are not.

But the only way we can decide which circumstances are morally relevant is to ask ourselves what would be the *consequences* of embodying those circumstances *in a general rule.* Thus we can relevantly say that it is the duty not only of A, but of *anybody* in financially comfortable circumstances, to pay for a college education for his own son. But we cannot relevantly say that it is not only the duty of A, but also of *anybody else* in a similarly financially comfortable situation, to pay for the college education of A's son. We can relevantly say that it is right not only for A, but for everyone, to tell a lie *if he has to do so to save a life;* but we cannot relevantly say that it is right not only for A, but for everyone, to tell a lie on Thursday night.[2]

In brief, the extent to which a moral rule or a duty should be generalized or particularized can only be determined by the social consequences that generalization or particularization would tend to have. And this once more points to the unsatisfactoriness of Kant's formulation of the principle of universalizability. It is valid (insofar as it insists that no one is entitled to treat himself as an exception), but it is not of much use. It tells us only that what is a moral rule for A is a moral rule for B or for anybody, that what is a duty for A is a duty for B or for anybody else *in those circumstances.* But it gives us no hint of how we are to test the validity or expediency of one moral rule as against another, or of what our particular duty *is* in particular circumstances.

A practical problem for which it is even more difficult to draw specific rules is: When someone fails, for any reason, to perform his or her specific duty, *whose* duty is it to substitute? If a mother and father fail in their duties to their own children, and allow them to go hungry or carelessly expose them to some contagious disease, whose duty is it to try to rectify the situation? The common law finds no solution to this problem, and common sense morality gives no definite answer.

4. The Choice of Vocation

But it is clear from the foregoing discussion that our special duties of relation and circumstance tend to merge with our special duties of vocation. Let us therefore return to our consideration of the latter.

Once we have adopted a vocation, we have either implicitly or explicitly adopted the special duties and risks that attend it. But this brings us to the problem: Have we any duty to adopt one vocation rather than another? Does each of us have one "true" vocation? Are we obliged to follow it? And how are we to determine what it is?

Obviously within a very wide range the choice of a trade or profession (when it is not more or less forced on us, as it often is) is a decision to be made mainly on economic grounds and on grounds of personal taste and preference. Within this wide range moral considerations cannot be said to enter. Yet the "duty" of choosing a profession has been called by one writer "the most important of all duties."[3] Certainly it is *one* of the most important decisions, and sometimes *the* most important, that each of us makes in his life. To what extent do or should moral considerations enter into this decision?

It is obvious that they must certainly enter in a negative sense. Nobody can excuse himself for a life of crime by declaring that he decided to adopt it because he thought this the quickest way to make a living, or because he had a special taste or talent for that kind of life. And even when we come to occupations that are within the law, many men will refuse even to consider going into a business that they feel to be ignoble or disreputable. Other men will feel that they have a positive "calling" or a positive duty to take up, say, the ministry or medicine.

We have said enough to indicate that the choice of a profession or vocation, though within certain limits it may be morally indifferent, must often involve a moral choice. Most of us recognize, in our judgments on our friends or on public figures, that a man owes a special obligation to his own gifts. Of the men whom we find throwing away their lives in drunkenness and dissipation, we condemn far more strongly a man whom we consider to be a great potential artist, scientist or writer, than one who has never shown any particular talent at all. We say of the former that he has sinned against his own talents. We are apt to be intolerant even of a mild laziness in him.

This may seem unjust and paradoxical. But common sense

morality is right in recognizing that special talents do impose special duties. For it recognizes that when such talents are unused, humanity loses far more than it does from the idleness or dissipation of mediocrities.

A man, then, has a duty to his own talents. He has a duty not to underestimate them, if this underestimate leads him to set his sights too low. "A man's reach should exceed his grasp." But only slightly. It is almost an equal sin for a man to over-estimate his talents when it leads him into ambitious projects at which he cannot succeed rather than into a more modest but more useful career. It is the latter possibility that is today more often forgotten or neglected. If one were to judge from the bulk of novels and plays on this theme in the last generation, the world is full of men who would have made great novelists or artists but were forced by their in-laws to go into the advertising business instead. Yet the real truth seems to be that America has a surplus of incompetent novelists and painters who, given the true nature and level of their talents, might at least have made useful and successful advertising-copy writers or illustrators.

If a man does have a duty to his talents, however, and I am assuming he does, this implies that special talents impose special duties. These duties rest on two grounds. We assume that a man who does not fully employ his talents will be unhappy. And if it is a duty of all of us to maximize the *general* happiness, then those whose powers enable them to make a greater contribution must have a greater obligation.

But does this not also have its reverse side? Does the genius who is the slave of his talent not have in compensation certain immunities from the duties of ordinary men? Does he have the right, for example, to abandon his wife and children to pursue his chosen work—or is he bound, like the rest of us, to the obligations he assumed by his earlier choice?

I shall not attempt here to answer this question, which has fascinated many novelists and dramatists (Somerset Maugham in *The Moon and Sixpence,* Bernard Shaw in *The Doctor's Dilemma,* Joyce

Cary in *Herself Surprised, The Horse's Mouth,* etc.), but I can make
one generalization. We have said that the great test of the morality
of actions is their tendency to promote or contribute toward social
cooperation. But an individual can sometimes cooperate best in the
long run by declining all but the most imperative family duties and
appeals for cooperation in specific "good causes" in order to con-
centrate all his time and energies on something that he alone can do,
or at least on something that he can do superlatively well—writing,
painting, composing, scientific research, or whatnot. The moral
judgment that we pass on him will depend both on whether his
neglect of the ordinary duties and decencies was really necessary to
his end, and whether we decide that he really was a genius, or only a
mediocrity afflicted with megalomania.

5. Summary

To sum up, then: A large part of human duty consists of acts
that are not the duty of everybody. There is and must be a division
and specialization of duty as there is and must be division and specialization of labor. This is not merely an analogy: the one implies
the other. Because we have to assume the full duties and responsibilities of our particular job, we are unable to take over the duties or
responsibilities of other jobs. Most of an educator's duties are confined not merely to education, but to the education of his particular
students in his particular subject, and not to other students or even
to his own students in other subjects. A policeman cannot even be
held responsible for the efficiency of a police department outside his
own precinct, let alone for the efficiency of the fire department, or
the efficiency of the fire department in another city.

And apart from the division and specialization of duty as the
result of the division and specialization of labor, our duty is also
limited and defined by our special talents, and by the vicinity, the
relation, the particular circumstances, place, or "station" in which
we find ourselves. It is because some of us have these special duties

that others are relieved of them. This is precisely what we mean when we say that everyone has his own inescapable *personal* responsibilities, which he cannot foist on others.

This does not mean, of course, that there are no universal duties. *Everyone* has a duty to speak the truth, to keep his promises and agreements, to act honorably. And even much particularity of duties (as we saw on page 98 can be reconciled with universality. But *every* act does not depend for justification on its universalizability. Some courses (such as voluntary celibacy) can quite properly, in fact, only be chosen by some on condition of their not being chosen by all.

And if we ask how we are to know our special duties, apart from those that inhere in the special vocation we have chosen, we are brought back for answer to two very old maxims, which may profitably be combined into one: Know thyself and Be thyself.

From our discovery of the necessary specialization of many duties we can come to a further conclusion. Our duties are not bottomless and endless. If the duties of each of us are specialized, they are also limited. No man is required to take the burdens of all mankind on his shoulders.

Many moral writers tell us that, "A man's duty under all circumstances is to do what is most conducive to the general good."[4] But this should not be interpreted as imposing on us the duty of trying to relieve the distress of everybody in the world, whether in India, China, or Upper Chad. The weight of such limitless duties, if we assumed we had them, would make us all feel constantly inadequate, guilty, and miserable. It would distract us from properly fulfilling our duties to ourselves and our immediate family, friends, and neighbors. These limited duties are as much as we can reasonably call upon most men to perform. Any generosity or dedication beyond that is optional, to be admired but not exacted. The professional do-gooders now rushing about the world, meddling in everybody's affairs, and constantly exhorting the rest of us that we are forgetting the wretchedness and poverty in Bolivia, Burma, or

Brazil, and that we are relaxing, playing or laughing when somebody is suffering or dying somewhere, make a very dubious contribution to the betterment of the human lot.

The principal real duties of the average man are, after all, not excessively onerous or demanding. They are to do his own job well, to treat his family with love, his intimates with kindness, and everyone with courtesy, and apart from that not to meddle in other people's affairs. A man who does this much is in fact cooperating with his fellows, and very effectively. If everyone did as much, the lot of man might still be far from perfect, but it would show infinite improvement over its present state.

---

1. *Selected Letters of Albert Jay Nock,* collected and edited by Francis J. Nock (Caldwell, Idaho: Caxton, 1962), p. 30.

2. See John Hospers' discussion of "The Principle of Relevant Specificity," in *Human Conduct,* pp. 320–322.

3. Hastings Rashdall, who endorses the statement, attributes it to Sir John Seeley. See Rashdall's *The Theory of Good and Evil,* II, p. 113.

4. E.g., Hastings Rashdall, *op. cit.,* II, 135.

CHAPTER 12

Rights

1. Legal Rights

The concept of Rights is in origin a legal concept. In fact, in most European languages the term for Law is identical with the term for Right. The Latin *jus,* the French *droit,* the Italian *diritto,* the Spanish *derecho,* the German *Recht* signify both the legal rule that binds a person and the legal right that every person claims as his own. These coincidences are no mere accident. Law and Right are correlative terms. They are two sides of the same coin. All private rights are derived from the legal order, while the legal order involves the aggregate of all the rights coordinated by it. As one legal writer puts it: "We can hardly define a right better than by saying that it is the *range of action assigned to a particular will within the social order established by law.*"[1]

In other words, just because every person under the rule of law is divested of an unlimited liberty of action, a certain liberty of action *within* the legal limits is conceded and guaranteed to him by right.

When a man claims something as a right, he claims it as *his own* or as *due to him.* The very conception of a legal right for one man implies an *obligation* on the part of somebody else or of everybody else. If a creditor has a right to a sum of money owed to him on a certain day, the debtor has an obligation to pay it. If you have a right to freedom of speech, to privacy, or to the ownership of a house, everyone else has an *obligation* to respect it. A legal right for me implies a legal duty of others not to interfere with my free exercise of it.

Among legal rights almost universally recognized and protected today are the right to freedom from assault or from arbitrary arrest or imprisonment, the right to be protected from arbitrary intrusion into one's home, the right to freedom of speech and publication (within certain established limits), the right to hold property, the right to compensation for damages inflicted by trespassers, the right to demand fulfillment of a contract, and many others.

The notion of legal right has its counterpart in legal duty. In their legal relations men either *claim* or *owe*. If A exerts an acknowledged right, he has the legal power to require that B (or that B, C, D, etc.) shall act or forbear to act in a certain way—shall do something or abstain from doing something.

Neither legally nor morally can "property rights" be properly contrasted with "human rights":

> The right of ownership is, strictly speaking, quite as much a personal right—the right of one person against other persons—as a right to service, or a lease. It may be convenient for certain purposes to speak of rights over things, but in reality there can only be rights *in respect of* things *against* persons. . . . Relations and intercourse arise exclusively between live beings; but goods as well as ideas are the object and the material of such relations; and when a right of ownership in a watch or a piece of land is granted to me by law, this means not only that the seller has entered into a personal obligation to deliver those things to me, but also that every person will be bound to recognize them as mine.[2]

"Every single legal rule may be thought of as one of the bulwarks or boundaries erected by society in order that its members shall not collide with each other in their actions."[3] As every legal rule appears as a necessary adjunct to some relation of social intercourse, it is often difficult to say whether the rule precedes the rights and duties involved in the relation, or vice versa. Both of these sides of law stand in constant cross-relations with each other.

In the last three centuries there has been an expansion of legal rights and an increasingly explicit recognition of their existence and importance. To protect the individual against abuses in statute law or by law-enforcement officials, "bills of rights" have been incorporated into written constitutions. The most famous of these is the Bill of Rights adopted in 1790 in the American Constitution.

The Bill of Rights is another name for the first Ten Amendments. It guarantees: freedom of worship, of speech, and of the press; the right of the people peaceably to assemble, and to petition the government for a redress of grievances; the right of the people to be secure in their persons, houses, papers, and effects, against unreasonable searches and seizures; the right of every person not to be compelled in any criminal case to be a witness against himself; nor to be deprived of life, liberty, or property, without due process of law; nor to have his property taken for public use, without just compensation; the right of the accused, in all criminal prosecutions, to a speedy and public trial by an impartial jury; the right to be protected against excessive bail and excessive fines, and cruel and unusual punishments.

This list is not complete. To the rights specified in the first Ten Amendments, additional rights were later added in the Fourteenth Amendment. Some rights, in fact, are specified in the original Constitution. The privilege of the writ of *habeas corpus* cannot be suspended unless in cases of rebellion or invasion or when the public safety may require it. Congress is prohibited from passing any bill of attainder or *ex post facto* law. Any State also is prohibited from passing any bill of attainder, *ex post facto law,* or law impairing the obligation of contracts.

2. Natural Rights

Especially in the last two centuries, there has been a broadening of the concept of legal rights to the notion of "natural" rights. This was already implicit and sometimes explicit, however, in the thought of Plato and Aristotle, of Cicero and the Roman jurists, and becomes more explicit and detailed in the writings of Locke, Rousseau, Burke, and Jefferson.[4]

The term *Natural Rights,* like the term *Natural Law,* is in some respects unfortunate. It has helped to perpetuate a *mystique* which regards such rights as having existed since the beginning of time; as having been handed down from heaven; as being simple, self-evident, and easily stated; as even being independent of the human will, independent of consequences, inherent in the nature of things. This concept is reflected in the Declaration of Independence: "We hold these truths to be self-evident, that all men are created equal, that they are endowed by their Creator with certain unalienable Rights, that among these are Life, Liberty, and the pursuit of Happiness."

Yet though the term *Natural Rights* easily lends itself to misinterpretation, the *concept* is indispensable; and it will do no harm to keep the term as long as we clearly understand it to mean *ideal* rights, the legal rights that every man *ought* to enjoy. The historic function of the doctrine of Natural Rights has been, in fact, to insist that the individual be guaranteed legal rights that he did not have, or held only uncertainly and precariously.

By a further extension, we are justified in talking not only of "natural" *legal* rights but of *moral* rights. Yet clarity of thought demands that we hold fast to at least one part of the *legal* meaning of "rights." We have seen that every right of one man implies a corresponding *obligation* of others to do something or refrain from doing something so that he may be protected in and even *guaranteed* that right. If we abandon this two-sided concept the term *right* becomes a mere rhetorical flourish without definite meaning.

3. Pseudo-Rights

Before we examine the real nature and function of "natural" or moral rights it will clarify our ideas to look at some illegitimate extensions of the concept.

These have been rife for the last generation. An outstanding example is the Four Freedoms announced by President Franklin D. Roosevelt in 1941. The first two of these—"freedom of speech and expression," and "freedom of every person to worship God in his own way"—are legitimate freedoms and legitimate rights. They were, in fact, already guaranteed in the Constitution. But the last two—"freedom from want . . . everywhere in the world" and "freedom from fear . . . anywhere in the world" are illegitimate extensions of the concept of freedom or the concept of rights.

It will be noticed that the first two are freedoms *of* (or *to*), and the second two are freedoms *from.* Had Roosevelt used the synonym "liberty," he would still have been able to promise "liberty *to,*" but English idiom would hardly have allowed him to promise "liberty *from.*"[5] "Freedom to" is a guaranty that no one, including the government, will be allowed to *interfere* with one's freedom of thought and expression; but "freedom *from*" means that it is considered the duty of *someone else* to supply one's wants or to *remove* one's fears. Aside from the fact that this is a demand impossible of fulfillment (in a world of daily dangers and in a world in which we have not collectively produced enough to meet all our wants), just how does it become someone else's duty to supply my wants or to banish my fears? And how do I decide just *whose* duty it is?

Another outstanding example of a demand for pseudo-rights is found in the Universal Declaration of Human Rights adopted by the General Assembly of the United Nations in 1948. This declaration states, for example, that "everyone has the right to rest and leisure, including reasonable limitation of working hours and periodic holidays with pay." Assuming that this is even possible for *everyone* (in South America, Asia, Africa, and in the present state of civilization), whose obligation is it to provide all this? And how far does each provider's alleged obligation extend?

The same questions may be asked of all the rhetorical demands for alleged rights that we now hear almost daily—"the right to a minimum standard of living"; "the right to a decent wage"; "the right to a job"; "the right to an education"; and even "the right to a *comfortable* living"; "the right to a *satisfactory* job," or "the right to a *good* education." It is not only that all these alleged rights have vague quantitative boundaries—that they do not specify how high a wage is considered "decent" or *how much* education "the right to an education" implies. What makes them pseudo-rights is that they imply that it is somebody else's obligation to supply those things. But they do not usually tell us *whose* obligation, or precisely how it comes to be *his*. My "right to a job" implies that it is somebody's else's *duty* to give me a job, apparently regardless of my qualifications or even whether I would do more damage than good on the job.

4. *Absolute* vs. *Prima Facie* Rights

Unfortunately, disposing of some of the more obviously pseudo-rights does only a little to simplify our problem. Natural rights or moral rights are not always self-evident, are not necessarily simple, and are seldom if ever absolute. If legal rights are the correlates of legal rules, moral rights are the correlates of moral rules. And as moral duties may sometimes conflict with each other, so may moral rights. My legal and moral rights are limited by your legal and moral rights. My right to freedom of speech, for example, is limited by your right not to be slandered. And "your right to swing your arm ends where my nose begins."

We must try to think of moral rights with at least as much care and precision as legislators, judges, and jurists are compelled to think of legal rights. We cannot be satisfied with any vague and easy rhetorical solutions. Legal rights actually constitute an intricate and interrelated structure of rights worked out by centuries of judicial reasoning applied to centuries of human experience. Contrary to Justice Holmes's facile epigram: "The life of the law has not been logic; it has been experience,"[6] the life of the law has been *both* logic and experience. The law is the product of logic and reason *brought to bear* on experience.

As everyone's rights are conditioned by the equal rights of others, as the rights of each must be harmonized and coordinated with the equal rights of all, and as one right may not always and everywhere be compatible with another, there are few if any *absolute* rights. Even the right to life and the right to freedom of speech are not absolute. John Locke often wrote as if the rights to life, liberty, and property *were* absolute, but he made exceptions and qualifications in the course of his discussion: "Every one as he is bound to preserve himself . . . so by the like reason, *when his own preservation comes not in competition,* ought he [do] as much as he can to preserve the rest of mankind, and not *unless it be to do justice on an offender,* take away or impair the life, or what tends to the preservation of the life, the liberty, health, limb, or goods of another."[7](My italics)

Even the right to freedom of speech does not extend to libel, slander, or obscenity (though there may be difficult problems of definition concerning the latter). And nearly everyone will concede the limits to free speech as defined by Justice Holmes in a celebrated opinion:

> The most stringent protection of free speech would not protect a man in falsely shouting fire in a theatre, and causing a panic. It does not even protect a man from injunction against uttering words that may have all the effect of force. The question in every case is whether the words are used in such circumstances and are of such a nature as to create a clear and present danger that they will bring about the substantive evils that Congress has a right to prevent. It is a question of proximity and degree.[8]

The suggestion has been made, following the analogy of the concept of *"prima facie* duties" (which we owe to Sir David Ross), that though we have no *absolute* rights, we do have *prima facie* rights. That is, we have a *prima facie* right to life, liberty, property, etc., which must be respected in the absence of some conflicting right or other consideration. But just as the law must be more precise than this, so must moral philosophy. Legal rights are of course subject to certain conditions and qualifications. But *within* those necessary qualifications, legal rights are or ought to be *inviolable.* And so, of course, should moral rights be.

This inviolability does not rest on some mystical yet self-evident "law of nature." It rests ultimately (though it will shock many to hear this) on utilitarian considerations. But it rests, not on *ad hoc utilitism,* on expediency in any narrow sense, but on *rule*-utilism, on the recognition that the highest and only permanent utility comes from an unyielding adherence to *principle.* Only by the most scrupulous respect for each other's imprescriptible rights can we maximize social peace, order, and cooperation.

---

1. Paul Vinogradoff, *Common-Sense in Law,* pp. 61–62. I am here indebted to Vinogradoff's whole discussion of the nature of rights in positive law.

2. *Ibid.,* pp. 68–69.

3. *Ibid.,* p. 70.

4. A scholarly and illuminating history can be found in Leo Strauss, *Natural Right and History* (Chicago: University of Chicago Press, 1953).

5. See George Santayana, *Dominations and Powers* (New York: Scribner's, 1951), p. 58n.

6. Justice Oliver Wendell Holmes, Jr., *The Common Law* (1881).

7. John Locke, *Two Treatises of Civil Government* (1689), Book II, Chap. 2, Sec. 6.

8. *Schenck v. United States,* 249 U.S. 52.

CHAPTER 13

The Ethics of Capitalism

1. A Socialist Smear Word

It is commonly assumed that there is little relation between the ethical and the economic point of view, or between Ethics and Economics. But they are, in fact, intimately related. Both are concerned with human action,[1] human conduct,[2] human decision, human choice. Economics is a *description, explanation,* or *analysis* of the determinants, consequences, and implications of human action and human choice. But the moment we come to the *justification* of human actions and decisions, or to the question of what an action or decision *ought* to be, or to the question whether the consequences of this or that action or rule of action would be more *desirable* in the long run for the individual or the community, we have entered the realm of Ethics. This is also true the moment we begin to discuss the desirability of one economic *policy* as compared with another.

Ethical conclusions, in brief, cannot be arrived at independently of, or in isolation from, analysis of the economic consequences of institutions, principles, or rules of action. The economic ignorance of most ethical philosophers, and the common failure even of those who have understood economic principles to apply them to ethical problems (on the assumption that economic principles are either irrelevant or too materialistic and mundane to apply to such a lofty and spiritual discipline as Ethics), have stood in the way of progress in ethical analysis, and account in part for the sterility of so much of it.

There is hardly an ethical problem, in fact, without its economic aspect. Our daily ethical decisions are in the main economic decisions, and nearly all our daily economic decisions have, in turn, an ethical aspect.

113

Moreover, it is precisely around questions of economic organization that most ethical controversy turns today. The main challenge to our traditional "bourgeois" ethical standards and values comes from the Marxists, the socialists, and the Communists. What is under attack is the capitalist system; and it is attacked mainly on ethical grounds, as being materialistic, selfish, unjust, immoral, savagely competitive, callous, cruel, destructive. If the capitalistic system is really worth preserving, it is futile today to defend it merely on technical grounds (as being more productive, for example) unless we can show also that the socialist attacks on ethical grounds are false and baseless.

We find ourselves confronted at the very beginning of such a discussion with a serious semantic handicap. The very name of the system was given to it by its enemies. It was intended as a smear word. The name is comparatively recent. It does not appear in *The Communist Manifesto* of 1848 because Marx and Engels had not yet thought of it. It was not until half a dozen years later that either they or one of their followers had the happy idea of coining the word. It exactly suited their purposes. Capitalism was meant to designate an economic system that was run exclusively by and for the capitalists. It still keeps that built-in connotation. Hence it stands self-condemned. It is this name that has made capitalism so hard to defend in popular argument. The almost complete success of this semantic trick is a major explanation of why many people have been willing to die for Communism but so few have been willing to die for "capitalism."

There are at least half-a-dozen names for this system, any one of which would be more appropriate and more truly descriptive: the System of Private Ownership of the Means of Production, the Market Economy, the Competitive System, the Profit-and-Loss System, Free Enterprise, the System of Economic Freedom. Yet to try at this late date to discard the word Capitalism may not only be futile but quite unnecessary. For this intended smear word does at least unintentionally call attention to the fact that all economic improvement, progress, and growth is dependent upon capital accumulation—upon constant increase in the quantity and improvement in the quality of the tools of production—machinery, plant, and equipment. Now the capitalistic system does more to promote this growth than any alternative.

2. Private Property and Free Markets

Let us see what the basic institutions of this system are. We may subdivide them for convenience of discussion into (1) private property, (2) free markets, (3) competition, (4) division and combination of labor, and (5) social cooperation. As we shall see, these are not separate institutions. They are mutually dependent: each implies the other, and makes it possible.

Let us begin with private property. It is neither a recent nor an arbitrary institution, as some socialist writers would have us believe. Its roots go as far back as human history itself. Every child reveals a sense of property with regard to his own toys. Scientists are just beginning to realize the astonishing extent to which some sense or system of property rights or territorial rights prevails even in the animal world.

The question that concerns us here, however, is not the antiquity of the institution, but its utility. When a man's property rights are protected, it means that he is able to retain and enjoy in peace the fruits of his labor. This security is his main incentive, if not his only incentive, to labor itself. If anyone were free to seize what the farmer had sown, cultivated, and raised, the farmer would no longer have any incentive to sow or to raise it. If anyone were free to seize your house after you had built it, you would not build it in the first place. All production, all civilization, rests on recognition of and respect for property rights. A free enterprise system is impossible without security of property as well as security of life. Free enterprise is possible only within a framework of law and order and morality. This means that free enterprise presupposes morality; but, as we shall later see, it also helps to preserve and promote it.

The second basic institution of a capitalist economy is the free market. The free market means the freedom of everybody to dispose of his property, to exchange it for other property or for money, or to employ it for further production, on whatever terms he finds acceptable. This freedom is, of course, a corollary of private property. Private property necessarily implies the right of use for consumption or for further production, and the right of free disposal or exchange.

It is important to insist that private property and free markets are not separable institutions. A number of socialists, for example, think they can duplicate the functions and efficiencies of the free market by imitating the free market in a socialist system—that is, in a system in which the means of production are in the hands of the State.

Such a view rests on mere confusion of thought. If I am a government commissar selling something I don't really own, and you are another commissar buying it with money that really isn't yours, then neither of us really cares what the price is. When, as in a socialist or communist country, the heads of mines and factories, of stores and collective farms, are mere salaried government bureaucrats, who buy foodstuffs or raw materials from other bureaucrats and sell their finished products to still other bureaucrats, the so-called prices at which they buy and sell are mere bookkeeping fictions. Such bureaucrats are merely playing an artificial game called "free market." They cannot make a socialist system work like a free-enterprise system merely by imitating the so-called free-market feature while ignoring private property.

This imitation of a free-price system actually exists, in fact, in Soviet Russia* and in practically every other socialist or communist country. But insofar as this mock-market economy works— that is, insofar as it helps a socialist economy to function at all—it

---

*Ed. note, Hazlitt wrote this in 1963, long before Soviet Russia dissolved in 1991.

does so because its bureaucratic managers closely watch what commodities are selling for on free world markets, and artificially price their own in conformity. Whenever they find it difficult or impossible to do this, or neglect to do it, their plans begin to go more seriously wrong. Stalin himself once chided the managers of the Soviet economy because some of their artificially-fixed prices were out of line with those on the free world market.

I should like to emphasize that in referring to private property I am not referring merely to personal property in consumption goods, like a man's food, toothbrush, shirt, piano, home, or car. In the modern market economy private ownership of the means of production is no less fundamental. Such ownership is from one point of view a privilege; but it also imposes on the owners a heavy social responsibility. The private owners of the means of production cannot employ their property merely for their own satisfaction; they are forced to employ it in ways that will promote the best possible satisfaction of consumers. If they do this well, they are rewarded by profits, and a further increase in their ownership; if they are inept or inefficient, they are penalized by losses. Their investments are never safe indefinitely. In a free-market economy the consumers, by their purchases or refusals to purchase, daily decide afresh who shall own productive property and how much he shall own. The owners of productive capital are compelled to employ it for the satisfaction of other people's wants.[3] A privately-owned railway is as much "dedicated to a public purpose" as a government-owned railway. It is likely in fact to achieve such a purpose far more successfully, not only because of the rewards it will receive for performing its task well, but even more because of the heavy penalties it will suffer if it fails to meet the needs of shippers or travelers at competitive costs and prices.

3. Competition

The foregoing discussion already implies the third integral institution in the capitalist system—competition. Every competitor in a private-enterprise system must meet the market price. He must keep his unit production costs below this market price if he is to survive. The further he can keep his costs below the market price the greater his profit margin. The greater his profit margin the more he will be able to expand his business and his output. If he is faced with losses for more than a short period he cannot survive. The effect of competition, therefore, is to take production constantly out of the hands of the less competent managers and put it more and more into the hands of the more efficient managers. Putting the matter in another way, free competition constantly promotes more and more efficient methods of production: it tends constantly to reduce production costs. As the lowest-cost producers expand their output they cause a reduction of prices and so force the highest-cost producers to sell their product at a lower price, and ultimately either to reduce their costs or to transfer their activities to other lines.

But capitalistic or free-market competition is seldom merely competition in lowering the cost of producing a homogeneous product. It is almost always competition in improving a specific product. And in the last century it has been competition in introducing and perfecting entirely new products or means of production—the railroad, the dynamo, the electric light, the motor car, the airplane, the telegraph, the telephone, the phonograph, the camera, motion pictures, radio, television, refrigerators, air conditioning, an endless variety of plastics, synthetics, and other new materials. The effect has been enormously to increase the amenities of life and the material welfare of the masses. Capitalistic competition, in brief, is the great spur to improvement and innovation, the chief stimulant to research, the principal incentive to cost reduction, to the development of new and better products, and to improved efficiency of every kind. It has conferred incalculable blessings on mankind.

And yet, in the last century, capitalistic competition has been under constant attack by socialists and anti-capitalists. It has been denounced as savage, selfish, cutthroat, and cruel. Some writers, of whom Bertrand Russell is typical, constantly talk of business competition as if it were a form of "warfare," and practically the same thing as the competition of war. Nothing could be more false or absurd—unless we think it reasonable to compare competition in mutual slaughter with competition in providing consumers with new or better goods and services at cheaper prices.

The critics of business competition not only shed tears over the penalties it imposes on inefficient producers but are indignant at the "excessive" profits it grants to the most successful and efficient. This weeping and resentment exist because the critics either do not understand or refuse to understand the function that competition performs for the consumer and therefore for the national welfare. Of course there are isolated instances in which competition seems to work unjustly. It sometimes penalizes amiable or cultivated people and rewards churlish or vulgar ones. No matter how good our system of rules and laws, isolated cases of injustice can never be entirely eliminated. But the beneficence or harmfulness, the justice or injustice, of institutions must be judged by their effect in the great majority of cases—by their overall result. We shall return to this point later.

What those who indiscriminately deplore "competition" overlook is that everything depends upon what the competition is in, and the nature of the means it employs. Competition *per se* is neither moral nor immoral. It is neither necessarily beneficial nor necessarily harmful. Competition in swindling or in mutual slaughter is one thing; but competition in philanthropy or in excellence—the competition between a Leonardo da Vinci and a Michelangelo, between a Shakespeare and a Ben Jonson, a Haydn and a Mozart, a Verdi and a Wagner, a Newton and a Leibnitz, is quite another. Competition does not necessarily imply relations of enmity, but relations of rivalry, of mutual emulation and mutual stimulation. Beneficial competition is indirectly a form of cooperation.

Now what the critics of economic competition overlook is that—when it is conducted under a good system of laws and a high standard of morals—it is itself a form of economic cooperation, or rather, that it is an integral and necessary part of a system of economic cooperation. If we look at competition in isolation, this statement may seem paradoxical, but it becomes evident when we step back and look at it in its wider setting. General Motors and Ford are not cooperating directly with each other; but each is trying to cooperate with the consumer, with the potential car buyer. Each is trying to convince him that it can offer him a better car than its competitor, or as good a car at a lower price. Each is "compelling" the other—or, to state it more accurately, each is stimulating the other—to reduce its production costs and to improve its car. Each, in other words, is "compelling" the other to cooperate more effectively with the buying public. And so, *indirectly,—triangularly,* so to speak— General Motors and Ford cooperate. Each makes the other more efficient.

Of course this is true of all competition, even the grim competition of war. As Edmund Burke put it: "He that wrestles with us strengthens our nerves and sharpens our skill. Our antagonist is our helper." But in free-market competition, this mutual help is also beneficial to the whole community.

For those who still think this conclusion paradoxical, it is merely necessary to consider the artificial competition of games and sport. Bridge is a competitive card game, but it requires the cooperation of four people in consenting to play with each other; a man who refuses to sit in to make a fourth is considered noncooperative rather than noncompetitive. To have a football game requires the cooperation not only of eleven men on each side but the cooperation of each side with the other—in agreeing to play, in agreeing on a given date, hour, and place, in agreeing on a referee, and in agreeing to abide by a common set of rules. The Olympic games would not be possible without the cooperation of the participating nations. There have been some very dubious analogies in the economic literature of recent years between economic life and "the theory of games"; but the analogy which recognizes that in both fields competition exists within a larger setting of cooperation (and that desirable results follow), is valid and instructive.

4. The Division of Labor

I come now to the fourth institution I have mentioned as part of the capitalist system—the division and combination of labor. The necessity and beneficence of this was sufficiently emphasized by the founder of political economy, Adam Smith, who made it the subject of the first chapter of his great work, *The Wealth of Nations.* In the very first sentence of that great work, indeed, we find Adam Smith declaring: "The greatest improvement in the productive powers of labor, and the greater part of the skill, dexterity, and judgment with which it is anywhere directed or applied, seem to have been the effects of the division of labor."[4]

Smith goes on to explain how the division and subdivision of labor leads to improved dexterity on the part of individual workers, in the saving of time commonly lost in passing from one sort of work to another, and in the invention and application of specialized machinery. "It is the great multiplication of the productions of all the different arts, in consequence of the division of labor," he concludes, "which occasions, in a well-governed society, that universal opulence which extends itself to the lowest ranks of the people."[5]

Nearly two centuries of economic study have only intensified this recognition. "The division of labor extends by the realization that the more labor is divided the more productive it is."[6] "The fundamental facts that brought about cooperation, society, and civilization and transformed the animal man into a human being are the facts that work performed under the division of labor is more productive than isolated work and that man's reason is capable of recognizing this truth."[7]

5. Social Cooperation

Though I have put division of labor ahead of social cooperation, it is obvious that they cannot be considered apart. Each implies the other. No one can specialize if he lives alone and must provide for all his own needs. Division and combination of labor already imply social cooperation. They imply that each exchanges part of the special product of his labor for the special product of the labor of others. But division of labor, in turn, increases and intensifies social cooperation. As Adam Smith put it: "The most dissimilar geniuses are of use to one another; the different produces of their respective talents, by the general disposition to truck, barter, and exchange, being brought, as it were, into a common stock, where every man may purchase whatever part of the produce of other men's talents he has occasion for."[8]

Modern economists make the interdependence of division of labor and social cooperation more explicit: "Society is concerted action, cooperation. . . . It substitutes collaboration for the—at least conceivable—isolated life of individuals. Society is division of labor and combination of labor. . . . Society is nothing but the combination of individuals for cooperative effort."[9]

Adam Smith also recognized this clearly:

> In civilized society [Man] stands at all times in need of the cooperation and assistance of great multitudes, while his whole life is scarce sufficient to gain the friendship of a few persons. . . . Man has almost constant occasion for the help of his brethren, and it is in vain for him to expect it from their benevolence only. He will be more likely to prevail if he can interest their self-love in his favor, and show them it is for their own advantage to do for him what he requires of them. Whoever offers to another a bargain of any kind, proposes to do this: Give me that which I want, and you shall have this which you want, is the meaning of every such offer; and it is in this manner that we obtain from one another the far greater part of those good offices which we stand in need of. It is not from the benevolence of the butcher, the brewer, or the baker, that we expect our dinner, but from their regard to their own interest. We address ourselves, not to

their humanity but to their self- love, and never talk to them of our own necessities but of their advantages.[10]

What Adam Smith was pointing out in this and other passages is that the market economy is as successful as it is because it takes advantage of self-love and self-interest and harnesses them to production and exchange. In an even more famous passage, Smith pressed the point further:

> The annual revenue of every society is always precisely equal to the exchangeable value of the whole annual produce of the industry, or rather is precisely the same thing with that exchangeable value. As every individual, therefore, endeavors as much as he can both to employ his capital in the support of domestic industry, and so to direct that industry that its produce may be of the greatest value; every individual necessarily labors to render the annual revenue of the society as great as he can. He generally, indeed, neither intends to promote the public interest, nor knows how much he is promoting it. By preferring the support of domestic to that of foreign industry, he intends only his own security; and by directing that industry in such a manner as its produce may be of the greatest value, he intends only his own gain, and he is in this, as in many other cases, led by an invisible hand to promote an end which was no part of his intention. Nor is it always the worse for the society that it was no part of it. By pursuing his own interest he frequently promotes that of the society more efficiently than when he really intends to promote it.[11]

This passage has become almost too famous for Smith's own good. Scores of writers who have heard nothing but the metaphor "an invisible hand" have misinterpreted or perverted its meaning.

They have taken it (though he used it only once) as the essence of the whole doctrine of *The Wealth of Nations*. They have interpreted it as meaning that Adam Smith, as a Deist, believed that the Almighty interfered in some mysterious way to insure that all self-regarding actions would lead to socially beneficial ends. This is clearly a misinterpretation. "The fact that the market provides for the welfare of each individual participating in it is a *conclusion* based on scientific analysis, not an assumption upon which the analysis is based."[12]

Other writers have interpreted the "invisible hand" passage as a defense of selfishness, and still others as a confession that a free-market economy is not only built on selfishness but rewards selfishness alone. And Smith was at least partly to blame for this latter interpretation. He failed to make explicit that only insofar as people earned their livings *in legal and moral ways* did they promote the general interest. People who try to improve their own fortunes by chicanery, swindling, robbery, blackmail, or murder do not increase the national income. Producers increase the national welfare by competing to satisfy the needs of consumers at the cheapest price. A free economy can function properly only within an appropriate legal and moral framework.

And it is a profound mistake to regard the actions and motivations of people in a market economy as necessarily and narrowly selfish. Though Adam Smith's exposition was brilliant, it could easily be misinterpreted. Fortunately, at least a few modern economists have further clarified the process and the motivation: The economic life " . . . consists of all that complex of relations into which we enter with other people, and lend ourselves or our resources to the furtherance of their purposes, as an indirect means of furthering our own."[13] Our own purposes are necessarily our *own;* but they are not necessarily purely *selfish* purposes. "The economic relation . . . or business nexus, is necessary alike for carrying on the life of the peasant and the prince, of the saint and the sinner, of the apostle and the

shepherd, of the most altruistic and the most egoistic of men. . . .
Our complex system of economic relations puts us in command of
the cooperation necessary to accomplish our purposes."[14]

"The specific characteristic of an economic relation," according
to Wicksteed, "is not its 'egoism,' but its 'non-tuism.'"[15] He
explains:

> If you and I are conducting a transaction which on my
> side is purely economic, I am furthering your purposes,
> partly or wholly perhaps for my own sake, perhaps entirely
> for the sake of others, but certainly not for your sake. What
> makes it an economic transaction is that I am not consider-
> ing you except as a link in the chain, or considering your
> desires except as the means by which I may gratify those of
> some one else—not necessarily myself. The economic rela-
> tion does not exclude from mind everyone but me, it poten-
> tially includes every one but you.[16]

There is a certain element of arbitrariness in making "non-
tuism" the essence of "the economic relation."[17] The element of
truth in this position is merely that a "strictly economic" relation is
by definition an "impersonal" relation. But one of Wicksteed's great
contributions was to dispose of the persistent idea that economic
activity is exclusively egoistic or self-regarding.[18] The real basis of
all economic activity is *cooperation.* As Mises has put it:

> Within the frame of social cooperation there can emerge
> between members of society feelings of sympathy and
> friendship and a sense of belonging together. These feelings
> are the source of man's most delightful and most sublime
> experiences . . . . However, they are not, as some have
> asserted, the agents that have brought about social relation-
> ships. They are fruits of social cooperation, they thrive only

within its frame; they did not precede the establishment of social relations and are not the seed from which they spring. . . .

[T]he characteristic feature of human society is purposeful cooperation. . . . Human society . . . is the outcome of a purposeful utilization of a universal law determining cosmic becoming, viz., the higher productivity of the division of labor. . . .

Every step by which an individual substitutes concerted action for isolated action results in an immediate and recognizable improvement in his conditions. The advantages derived from peaceful cooperation and division of labor are universal. They immediately benefit every generation and not only later descendants. For what the individual must sacrifice for the sake of society he is amply compensated by greater advantages. His sacrifice is only apparent and temporary; he foregoes a smaller gain in order to reap a greater one later. . . . When social cooperation is intensified by enlarging the field in which there is division of labor or when legal protection and the safeguarding of peace are strengthened, the incentive is the desire of all those concerned to improve their own conditions. In striving after his own—rightly understood—interests the individual works toward an intensification of social cooperation and peaceful intercourse. . . .

The historical role of the theory of the division of labor as elaborated by British political economy from Hume to Ricardo consisted in the complete demolition of all metaphysical doctrines concerning the origin and operation of social cooperation. It consummated the spiritual, moral and intellectual emancipation of mankind inaugurated by the philosophy of Epicureanism. It substituted an autonomous rational morality for the heteronomous and intuitionist ethics of older days. Law and legality, the moral code and social institutions are no longer revered as unfathomable decrees of Heaven. They are of human origin, and the only yardstick that must be applied to them is that of expediency with regard to human welfare. The utilitarian economist does not say: Fiat justitia, pereat mundus.[a] He says: Fiat justitia, *ne* pereat mundus.[b] He does not ask a man to renounce his well-being for the benefit of society. He advises him to recognize what his rightly understood interests are.[19]

Mises expounded the same point of view in his earlier book, *Socialism*. Here also, and in contradiction to the Kantian thesis that it is wrong ever to treat others merely as means, he emphasizes the same theme that we have seen in Wicksteed:

[L]iberal social theory proves that each single man sees in all others, first of all, only means to the realization of his purposes, while he himself is to all others a means to the realization of their purposes; that finally, by this reciprocal action, in which each is simultaneously means and end, the highest aim of social life is attained—the achievement of a better existence for everyone. As society is only possible if everyone, while living his own life, at the same time helps others to live, if every individual is simultaneously means and end; if each individual's well-being is simultaneously the condition necessary to the well-being of the others, it is evident that the contrast between I and thou, means and end, automatically is overcome.[20]

Once we have recognized the fundamental principle of social cooperation, we find the true reconciliation of "egoism" and "altruism." Even if we assume that everyone lives and wishes to live primarily for himself, we can see that this does not disturb social life but promotes it, because the higher fulfillment of the individual's

---

a. "Let justice be done, (though) the world be destroyed."
b. "Let justice be done, (so) the world will not be destroyed."

life is possible only in and through society. In this sense egoism could be accepted as the basic law of society. But the basic fallacy is that of assuming a necessary incompatibility between "egoistic" and "altruistic" motives, or even of insisting on a sharp distinction between them. As Mises puts it:

> This attempt to contrast egoistic and altruistic action springs from a misconception of the social interdependence of individuals. The power to choose whether my actions and conduct shall serve myself or my fellow beings is not given to me— which perhaps may be regarded as fortunate. If it were, human society would not be possible. In the society based on division of labor and cooperation, the interests of all members are in harmony, and it follows from this basic fact of social life that ultimately action in the interests of myself and action in the interests of others do not conflict, since the interests of individuals come together in the end. Thus the famous scientific dispute as to the possibility of deriving the altruistic from the egoistic motives of action may be regarded as definitely disposed of.
>
> There is no contrast between moral duty and selfish interests. What the individual gives to society to preserve it as society, he gives, not for the sake of aims alien to himself, but in his own interest.[21]

This social cooperation runs throughout the free-market system. It exists between producer and consumer, buyer and seller. Both gain from the transaction, and that is why they make it. The consumer gets the bread he needs; the baker gets the monetary profit which is both his stimulus to bake the bread and the necessary means to enable him to bake more. In spite of the enormous labor-union and socialist propaganda to the contrary, the relation of employer and employed is basically a cooperative relation. Each needs the other. The more efficient the employer, the more workers he can hire and the more he can offer them. The more efficient the workers, the more each can earn, and the more successful the employer. It is in the interest of the employer that his workers should be healthy and vigorous, well fed and well housed, that they should feel they are being justly treated, that they will be rewarded in proportion to their efficiency and that they will therefore strive to be efficient. It is in the interest of the worker that the firm for which he works can do so at a profit, and preferably at a profit that both encourages and enables it to expand.

On the "microeconomic" scale, every firm is a cooperative enterprise. A magazine or a newspaper (and as one who has been associated with newspapers and magazines all his working life I can speak with immediate knowledge of this) is a great cooperative organization in which every reporter, every editorial writer, every advertising solicitor, every printer, every delivery-truck driver, every newsdealer, cooperates to play his assigned part, in the same way as an orchestra is a great cooperative enterprise in which each player cooperates in an exact way with his particular instrument to produce the final harmony. A great industrial company, such as General Motors, or the U. S. Steel Corporation, or General Electric—or, for that matter, any of a thousand others—is a marvel of continuous cooperation. And on a "macroeconomic" scale, the whole free world is bound together in a system of international cooperation through mutual trade, in which each nation supplies the needs of others cheaper and better than the others could supply their own needs acting in isolation. And this cooperation takes place, both on the smallest and on the widest scale, because each of us finds that forwarding the purposes of others is (though indirectly) the most effective of all means for achieving his own.

Thus, though we may call the chief drive "egoism," we certainly cannot call this a purely egoistic or "selfish" system. It is the system by which each of us tries to achieve his purposes whether those purposes are "egoistic" or "altruistic." The system certainly cannot be called dominantly "altruistic," because each of us is cooperating with others, not primarily to forward the purposes of those others, but primarily to forward his own. The system might most appropriately be called "mutualistic." In any case, its primary requirement is cooperation.

6. Is Capitalism Unjust?

Let us turn now to another consideration. Is the free-market system, the "capitalist" system, just or unjust? Virtually the whole burden of the socialist attack on the "capitalist" system is its alleged injustice—its alleged "exploitation" of the worker. A book on ethics is not the place to examine that contention fully. Such an examination is a task of economics. I hope the reader will forgive me, therefore, if, instead of examining this socialist argument directly, I merely accept the conclusion of John Bates Clark, in his epoch-making work, *The Distribution of Wealth* (1899) and refer the reader to that and other works on economics[22] or the supporting arguments for his conclusion.

The general thesis of Clark's work is that, "Free competition tends to give to labor what labor creates, to capitalists what capital creates, and to entrepreneurs what the coordinating function creates. . . . [It tends] to give to each producer the amount of wealth that he specifically brings into existence."[23]

Clark argues, in fact, that the tendency of a free competitive system is to give "to each what he creates." If this is true, he continues, it not only disposes of the exploitation theory, that "workmen are regularly robbed of what they produce," but it means that the capitalist system is essentially a just system, and that our effort should be, not to destroy it and substitute another utterly different in kind, but to perfect it so that exceptions to its prevalent rule of distribution may be less frequent and less considerable.[24]

Certain qualifications must be made in these conclusions. As Clark himself points out, this principle of "distribution"[25] in the free market represents a *tendency*. It does not follow that *in every instance* everyone gets exactly the value of what he has produced or helped to produce. And the value of his contribution that he gets is the *market* value—i.e., the value of that contribution *as measured by others.*

But whatever the shortcomings of this system may be from the requirements of perfect justice, no superior system has yet been conceived.

But before we come to our final moral evaluation of this marvelous free-market system, we must notice one other great virtue. It is not merely that it tends constantly to reward individuals in accordance with their specific contribution to production. By the constant play in the market of prices, wages, rents, interest rates, and other costs, relative profit margins or losses, the market tends constantly to achieve not only maximum production but optimum production. That is to say, through the incentives and deterrents provided by these ever-changing relationships of prices and costs, the production of thousands of different commodities and services is synchronized, and a dynamic balance is maintained in the volume of production of each of these thousands of different goods in relation to each other. This balance does not necessarily reflect the wishes of any one individual. It does not necessarily correspond with the utopian ideal of any economic planner. But it does tend to reflect the composite wishes of the whole existing body of producers and consumers. For each consumer, by his purchases or abstentions from purchase, daily casts his vote for the production of more of this commodity and less of that; and the producer is forced to abide by the consumers' decisions.[26]

Having seen what this system does, let us now look at the justice of it a little more closely. It is commonly regarded as "unjust" because the unthinking ideal of "social justice," from time immemorial, has been absolute equality of income. Socialists are never tired of condemning "poverty in the midst of plenty." They cannot rid themselves of the idea that the wealth of the rich is the cause of the poverty of the poor. Yet this idea is completely false. The wealth of the rich makes the poor less poor, not more. The rich are those who have something to offer in return for the services of the poor. And only the rich can provide the poor with the capital, with the tools of production, to increase the output and hence the marginal value of the labor of the poor. When the rich grow richer, the poor grow, not poorer, but richer. This, in fact, is the history of economic progress.

Any serious effort to enforce the ideal of equality of income, regardless of what anyone does or fails to do to earn or create income—regardless of whether he works or not, produces or not—would lead to universal impoverishment. Not only would it remove any incentive for the unskilled or incompetent to improve themselves, and any incentive for the lazy to work at all; it would remove even the incentive of the naturally talented and industrious to work or to improve themselves.

Justice is not purely an end in itself. It is not an ideal that can be isolated from its consequences. Though admittedly an intermediate end, it is primarily a means. Justice, in brief, consists of the social arrangements and rules that are most conducive to social cooperation—which means, in the economic field, most conducive to maximizing production. And the justice of these arrangements and rules, in turn, is not to be judged purely by their effect in this or that isolated instance, but (in accordance with the principle first pointed out by Hume) by their overall effect in the long run.

Practically all arguments for the equal distribution of income tacitly assume that such an equal division would do nothing to reduce the average income; that total income and wealth would remain at least as great as they would have been in a free-market system in which everyone was paid in accordance with his own production or his own contribution to production. This assumption is one of unsurpassable naïveté. Such an enforced equal division—and it could only be achieved by force—would cause a violent and disastrous drop in production and impoverish the nation that adopted it. Communist Russia was quickly forced to abandon this equalitarian idea; and to the extent that communist countries have tried to adhere to it, their people have paid dearly.

It may be supposed—and it is everywhere popularly supposed today—that there is some "third" system, some "middle-of-the-road" system, that could combine the enormous productivity of a free-market system with the "justice" of a socialist system—or that could, at least, bring a nearer equality of income and welfare than that produced in a completely free economic system. I can only state here my own conclusion that this is a delusion. If any such middle-of-the-road system did remedy a few specific injustices, it would do so only by creating many more—and incidentally by reducing total production compared with what a free-market system would achieve. For the basis of this conclusion I must refer the reader to treatises on economics.[27]

7. Is the Market "Ethically Indifferent"?

We come now, however, to a position very frequently taken by economists in recent decades, a position for which Philip H. Wicksteed, in his *Common Sense of Political Economy* (1910) may have helped to set the fashion. This is that the economic system is an "ethically indifferent instrument." Wicksteed argues for this position in a passage of great eloquence and penetration, from which I quote a substantial portion:

> We have now seen that the taint of inherent sordidness which attaches itself in many minds to the economic relation, or even to the study of it, is derived from a faulty conception of its nature. But, on the other hand, the easy optimism that expects the economic forces, if only we give them free play, spontaneously to secure the best possible conditions of life, is equally fallacious, and even more pernicious. It is, indeed, easy to present the working of the economic forces as wholly beneficent. Have we not seen that they automatically organize a vast system of cooperation, by

which men who have never seen or heard of each other, and who scarcely realize each other's existence or desires even in imagination, nevertheless support each other at every turn, and enlarge the realization each of the other's purposes? Do they not embrace all the world in one huge mutual benefit society? That London is fed day by day, although no one sees to it, is itself a fact so stupendous as to excuse, if it does not justify, the most exultant paeans that were ever sung in honor of the *laissez-faire laissez-passer* theory of social organization. What a testimony to the efficiency of the economic nexus is borne by the very fact that we regard it as abnormal that any man should perish for want of any one of a thousand things, no one of which he can either make or do for himself. When we see the world, in virtue of its millions of mutual adjustments, carrying itself on from day to day, and ask, "Who sees to it all?" and receive no answer, we can well understand the religious awe and enthusiasm with which an earlier generation of economists contemplated those "economic harmonies," in virtue of which each individual, in serving himself, of necessity serves his neighbor, and by simply obeying the pressures about him, and following the path that opens before him, weaves himself into the pattern of "purposes he cannot measure."

But we must look at the picture more closely. The very process of intelligently seeking my own ends makes me further those of others? Quite so. But what are my purposes, immediate and ultimate? And what are the purposes of others which I serve, as a means of accomplishing my own? And what views have I and they as to the suitable means of accomplishing those ends? These are the questions on which the health and vigor of a community depend, and the economic forces, as such, take no count of them. Division of labor and exchange, on which the economic organization of society is based, enlarge our means of accomplishing our ends, but they have no direct influence upon the ends themselves, and have no tendency to beget scrupulousness in the use of the means. It is idle to assume that ethically desirable results will necessarily be produced by an ethically indifferent instrument, and it is as foolish to make the economic relation an idol as it is to make it a bogey.

The world has many things that I want for myself and others, and that I can get only by some kind of exchange. What, then, have I, or what can I do or make, that the world wants? Or what can I make it want, or persuade it that it wants, or make it believe that I can give it better than others can? The things I want, if measured by an ideal standard, may be good or bad for me to have or for others to give; and so with the things I give them, the desires I stimulate in them, and the means I employ to gratify them. When we draw the seductive picture of "economic harmony" in which every one is "helping" some one else and making himself "useful" to him, we insensibly allow the idea of "help" to smuggle in with it ethical or sentimental associations that are strictly contraband. We forget that the "help" may be impartially extended to destructive and pernicious or to constructive and beneficent ends, and moreover that it may employ all sorts of means. We have only to think of the huge industries of war, of the floating of bubble companies, of the efforts of one business or firm to choke others in the birth, of the poppy culture in China and India, of the gin-palaces and distilleries at home, in order to realize how often the immediate purpose of one man or of one community is to thwart or hold in check the purpose of another, or to delude men, or to corrupt their tastes and to minister to them when corrupted.[28]

I have quoted Wicksteed at such great length because his is the most powerful statement I have ever encountered of the thesis that the free-market system is "ethically indifferent" or ethically neutral. The thesis, nevertheless, seems to me open to serious question.

Let us begin by confronting it with one or two statements of the rival thesis that the free-market economy does have a positive moral value. The reader will recall the passage from Ludwig von Mises already quoted on pages 125–127 in which he contends that "feelings of sympathy and friendship and a sense of belonging together . . . are fruits of social cooperation" and *not* the seed from which social cooperation springs. A similar contention is put forward by economist Murray N. Rothbard:

> In explaining the origins of society, there is no need to conjure up any mystic communion or "sense of belonging" among individuals. Individuals recognize, through the use of reason, the advantages of exchange resulting from the higher productivity of the division of labor, and they proceed to follow this advantageous course. In fact, it is far more likely that feelings of friendship and communion are the *effects* of a regime of (contractual) social co-operation rather than the cause. Suppose, for example, that the division of labor were not productive, or that men had failed to recognize its productivity. In that case, there would be little or no opportunity for exchange, and each man would try to obtain his goods in autistic independence. The result would undoubtedly be a fierce struggle to gain possession of the scarce goods, since, in such a world, each man's gain of useful goods would be some other man's loss. It would be almost inevitable for such an autistic world to be strongly marked by violence and perpetual war. Since each man could gain from his fellows only at their expense, violence would be prevalent, and it seems highly likely that feelings of mutual hostility would be dominant. As in the case of animals quarreling over bones, such a warring world could cause only hatred and hostility between man and man. Life

would be a bitter "struggle for survival." On the other hand, in a world of voluntary social co-operation through mutually beneficial exchanges, where one man's gain is another man's gain, it is obvious that great scope is provided for the development of social sympathy and human friendships. It is the peaceful, co-operative society that creates favorable conditions for feelings of friendship among men.

The mutual benefits yielded by exchange provide a major incentive . . . to would-be *aggressors* (initiators of violent action against others) to restrain their aggression and cooperate peacefully with their fellows. Individuals then decide that the advantages of engaging in specialization and exchange outweigh the advantages that war might bring.[29]

Let us now look a little more closely at Wicksteed's thesis. It is true, as he so eloquently points out, that capitalism, as it functioned in his time and today, is not yet a heaven filled with cooperating saints. But this does not prove that the system is responsible for our individual shortcomings and sins, or even that it is ethically "indifferent" or neutral. Wicksteed *took for granted* not only the economic but the ethical merits of the capitalism of his day because that was the system that he saw all round him, and therefore he did not visualize the alternative. What he forgot when he wrote the passage quoted above is that modern capitalism is not an inevitable or inescapable system but one that has been chosen by the men and women who live under it. It is a *system of freedom.* London is not fed "although no one sees to it." London is fed precisely because almost *everybody* in London sees to it. The housewife shops every day for food, and brings it home by car or on foot. The butcher and grocer know that she will shop, and stock what they expect her to buy. The meats and vegetables are brought to their shops in their own trucks or the trucks of wholesalers, who in turn order from shippers, who in turn order from farmers and order railroads to transport the food, and the railroads exist precisely to do that. All that is lacking in this system is a single dictator who ostentatiously issues commands for the whole thing and claims all the credit for it.

True, this system of freedom, this free-market system, presupposes an appropriate legal system and an appropriate morality. It could not exist and function without them. But once this system exists and functions it raises the moral level of the community still further.

8. The Function of Freedom

Wicksteed does not quite seem to have realized that in describing a market economy he was describing a system of economic *freedom,* and freedom is not "ethically indifferent," but a necessary condition of morality. As F. A. Hayek has put it:

> It is . . . an old discovery that morals and moral values will grow only in an environment of freedom, and that, in general, moral standards of people and classes are high only where they have long enjoyed freedom—and proportional to the amount of freedom they have possessed. . . . That freedom is the matrix required for the growth of moral values—indeed not merely one value among many but the source of all values—is almost self-evident. It is only where the individual has choice, and its inherent responsibility, that he has occasion to affirm existing values, to contribute to their further growth, and to earn moral merit.[30]

If the morality of a given free-market system falls short of perfection, this is no proof that the free-market system is ethically indifferent or ethically neutral. If a prior morality is necessary for it to come into existence, its existence nonetheless promotes a wider and more sustained morality. The habit of voluntary economic cooperation tends to make a mutualistic attitude habitual. And a system that provides us better than any other with our material needs and wants can never be dismissed as ethically negligible or ethically irrelevant. Morality depends upon the prior satisfaction of material needs. As Wicksteed himself so memorably put it in another context: "A man can be neither a saint, nor a lover, nor a poet, unless he has comparatively recently had something to eat."[31]

Ironically, precisely because capitalism does make it possible for men to meet their material needs, and often amply, it has been deplored as a "materialistic" system. To this an excellent answer has been given by F. A. Hayek: "Surely it is unjust to blame a system as more materialistic because it leaves it to the individual to decide whether he prefers material gain to other kinds of excellence, instead of having this decided for him. . . . If [a free enterprise society] gives individuals much more scope to serve their fellows by the pursuit of purely materialistic aims, it also gives them the opportunity to pursue any other aim they regard as more important."[32]

To which I may add that in a free economy everyone is free to practice generosity toward others to any extent he sees fit—and to any extent he is able to.

As voluntary economic cooperation makes us more interdependent, the consequences of breaches of cooperation or a breakdown of the system become more serious for all of us; and to the extent that we recognize this we will become less indifferent to failure or violation of cooperation in ourselves or in others. Therefore the tendency will be for the moral level of the whole community to be kept high or to be raised.

The way to appreciate the true moral value of the free-market economy is to ask ourselves: *If this freedom did not exist, what then?* We undervalue it, not only economically but morally, only because we have it and think it secure. As Shakespeare has put it:

> For it so falls out
> That what we have we prize not to the worth
> Whiles we enjoy it, but being lack'd and lost,
> Why, then we rack the value; then we find

The virtue that possession would not show us
Whiles it was ours.[33]

Writing in 1910, Wicksteed had an excuse which we do not have
for regarding the capitalist system as morally indifferent. He did not
have the stark alternatives before him. He had not been reading or
experiencing daily, for years, the results of statism, of government
economic planning, of socialism, of fascism, of communism.

To sum up: The system of capitalism, of the market economy, is
a system of freedom, of justice, of productivity. In all these respects
it is infinitely superior to its coercive alternatives. But these three
virtues cannot be separated. Each flows out of the other. Only when
men are free can they be moral. Only when they are free to choose
can they be said to choose right from wrong. When they are free to
choose, when they are free to get and to keep the fruits of their
labor, they feel that they are being treated justly. As they recognize
that their reward depends on their own efforts and output (and in
effect *is* their output) each has the maximum incentive to maximize
his output, and all have the maximum incentive to cooperate in
helping each other to do so. The justice of the system grows out of
the freedom it insures, and the productivity of the system grows out
of the justice of the rewards that it provides.

---

1. *Cf.* Ludwig von Mises, *Human Action,* a book on the principles of economics.

2. *Cf.* John Hospers, *Human Conduct,* a book on the principles of ethics.

3. *Cf.* Ludwig von Mises, *Human Action, Socialism* [see note 6 *infra*—Ed.],
etc.

4. Adam Smith, *The Wealth of Nations* (1776), Cannan ed. (New York: Modern Library, 1937), Book I. Chap. I. The phrase had already been used and the
theme stated in a passage in Mandeville's *Fable of the Bees,* 1729, II. Dialogue 6, p.
335.

The reader will notice a certain overlap and duplication in the quotations in
this chapter from Adam Smith and Philip Wicksteed and those from the same
authors in Chap. 3, "Social Cooperation." But I think these duplications are justified in the interests of emphasis and of saving the reader the inconvenience of turning back to that chapter to remind himself of the few sentences repeated here.

5. Adam Smith, *op. cit.,* p. 12.

6. Ludwig von Mises, *Socialism: An Economic and Sociological Analysis* trans. by J. Cahane, (London: J. Cape, 1936; New Haven: Yale, 1951), p. 299.

7. Ludwig von Mises, *Human Action,* p. 144.

8. Adam Smith, *op. cit.,* p. 16.

9. Ludwig von Mises, *Human Action,* p. 143.

10. Adam Smith, *op. cit.,* p. 14.

11. *Ibid.,* p. 423.

12. See Murray N. Rothbard, *Man, Economy, and State* (Princeton, N.J.: Van Nostrand, 1962), I, 440n. See also *ibid.,* I, 85–86.

13. Philip H. Wicksteed, *The Common Sense of Political Economy,* p. 158. The whole chapter on "Business and the Economic Nexus," from which this and later quotations are drawn, is a brilliant exposition that deserves the most careful study.

14. *Ibid.,* pp. 171, 172.

15. *Ibid.,* p. 180.

16. *Ibid.,* p. 174.

17. *Cf.* Israel M. Kirzner, *The Economic Point of View* (Princeton: Van Nostrand, 1960), p 66.

18. See Professor Lionel Robbins's Introduction to the 1933 edition of Wicksteed's *The Common Sense of Political Economy:* "Before Wicksteed wrote, it was still possible for intelligent men to give countenance to the belief that the whole structure of Economics depends upon the assumption of a world of economic men, each actuated by egocentric or hedonistic motives . . . . Wicksteed shattered this misconception once for all" (p. xxi).

19. Ludwig von Mises, *Human Action,* pp. 144–147.

20. Ludwig von Mises, *Socialism,* p. 432.

21. *Ibid.,* pp. 397–398.

22. *E.g.,* Eugen von Böhm-Bawerk, *Karl Marx and the Close of His System* (1896) (New York: Augustus M. Kelley, 1949); Ludwig von Mises, *Socialism* and *Human Action.* Practically the whole of modern economic literature, in its acceptance of the marginal productivity theory of wages, is in effect a refutation of the Marxist exploitation theory, and a substantial acceptance of the conclusions of J. B. Clark.

23. John Bates Clark, *The Distribution of Wealth* (1886) (New York: Kelley & Millman, 1956), pp. 3–4.

24. *Ibid.,* p. 9.

25. The older economic textbooks (i.e., of the late nineteenth and early twentieth centuries) commonly devoted separate chapters or even separate sections to "Production" and "Distribution" respectively. This was misleading. Wealth is not first "produced" and then "distributed." This is a socialist misconception. If a farmer raises a crop by himself he gets the whole crop because he has produced it.

It is not "distributed" to him; it is merely not taken away from him. If he sells it on the market, he gets the monetary market value of the crop in exchange just as a worker gets the monetary market value for his labor.

26. For a fuller description of this process, see Henry Hazlitt, "How the Price System Works" in *Economics in One Lesson.*

27. See especially the works of Ludwig von Mises, including his more popular *Planning for Freedom* (South Holland, Ill.: Libertarian Press, 1952), particularly the chapter, "Middle-of-the-Road Policy Leads to Socialism." I may refer interested readers also to my own *Economics in One Lesson.*

28. Philip H. Wicksteed, "Business and the Economic Nexus" (Chap. V), in *The Common Sense of Political Economy,* pp. 183-185.

29. Murray N. Rothbard, *op. cit.,* pp. 85-86.

30. F. A. Hayek, "The Moral Element in Free Enterprise," in *The Spiritual and Moral Significance of Free Enterprise* (New York: National Association of Manufacturers, 1961), pp. 26–27.

31. Philip H. Wicksteed, *The Common Sense,* p. 154.

32. F. A. Hayek, "The Moral Element in Free Enterprise," in *The Spiritual and Moral Significance of Free Enterprise* (New York: National Association of Manufacturers, 1961), pp. 32–33.

33. William Shakespeare, *Much Ado About Nothing,* Act IV, scene 1, line 219.

CHAPTER 14

The Ethics of Socialism

1. The Alternative to Freedom

In the preceding chapter we tried to confine ourselves to a discussion of the positive ethical values of "capitalism"—i.e., of the system of economic freedom. We did this because these values are so seldom appreciated or even considered. For more than a century the system has been under constant attack from numberless detractors (including those who owe most to it), and even the majority of its defenders have been apologetic about it, contenting themselves with pointing out that it is more productive than its alternatives.

This is a valid defense. It has, indeed, an ethical as well as a "merely material" validity. Capitalism has enormously raised the level of the masses. It has wiped out whole areas of poverty. It has greatly reduced infant mortality, and made it possible to cure disease and prolong life. It has reduced human suffering. Because of capitalism, millions live today who would otherwise have not even been born. If these facts have no ethical relevance, then it is impossible to say in what ethical relevance consists.

But though a defense of capitalism solely because of its productivity is valid and even ethically valid, it is not ethically sufficient. We cannot fully appreciate the positive ethical values of a system of economic freedom until we compare it with its alternatives.

So let us compare it now with its only real alternative— socialism. Some readers may object that there are any number of alternatives, a whole spectrum ranging from various degrees of interventionism and statism to communism. But to avoid getting into purely economic issues, I am going to be dogmatic at this point and say that all so-called middle-of-the-road systems are unstable and transitional in nature, and in the long run either break down or lead toward a complete socialism. For the argument in support of this conclusion, I must refer the reader to the relevant economic literature.[1] Here I will content myself with calling attention to the difference between a general indiscriminatory system of laws against force and fraud, on the one hand, and specific interventions in the market economy on the other. Some of these specific interventions may indeed "remedy" this or that specific "evil" in the short run, but they can do so only at the cost of producing more and worse evils in the long run.[2]

I should also warn the reader that in most of this discussion we shall be treating "socialism" and "communism" as practically synonymous. This was the practice of Marx and Engels. It is true that the words have come to have different connotations today; later in this chapter we shall recognize these. But in most of this discussion we shall assume, with Bernard Shaw, that "A communist is nothing but a socialist with the courage of his convictions." The parties and programs in present-day Europe that call themselves "socialist" in fact advocate merely a *partial* socialism—the nationalization of railroads, various public utilities, and heavy industry—but not usually of light industries, the service trades, or agriculture. When socialism becomes complete, it becomes what is generally called communism.

An additional distinction: the parties that call themselves Communist believe in getting into power, if necessary, through violent revolution, and in spreading their power by infiltration, hate-propaganda, subversion and war against other nations; whereas the parties that call themselves Socialist profess (for the most part sincerely) to wish to come into power only through persuasion and "democratic means." But we can leave a discussion of such differences until later.

2. Utopian Socialism

Let us begin by considering the ethical assumptions of utopian (or pre-Marxist) socialism. The utopian socialists have always deplored the alleged cruelty and savagery of economic competition, and have pleaded for the substitution of a regime of "cooperation" or "mutual aid." This plea rests, as we have seen in the preceding chapter, on a failure to understand that a free-market system is in fact a marvelous system of social cooperation, both on a "microeconomic" and on a "macroeconomic" scale. It rests on a failure to recognize, in addition, that economic competition is an integral and indispensable part of this system of economic cooperation, and enormously increases its effectiveness.

Utopian socialists constantly talk of the "wastefulness" of competition. They fail to understand that the apparent "wastes" of competition are short-term and transitional wastes necessary to increasing economies in the long run. One does not get any comparable long-run economies under monopolies. Above all, one does not get them under governmental monopolies: witness the post-office.

In *Looking Backward* (1888), the most famous utopian-socialist novel of the late nineteenth century, Edward Bellamy portrayed what he considered an ideal society. And one of the features that made it ideal was that it eliminated the

> interminable rows of stores [in Boston] . . . ten thousand stores to distribute the goods needed by this one city, which in my [utopian-socialist] dream had been supplied with all things from a single warehouse, as they were ordered through one great store in every quarter, where the buyer, without waste of time or labor, found under one roof the world's assortment in whatever line he desired. . . . All these ten thousand plants [stores] must be paid for, their rent, their staffs of superintendence, their platoons of salesmen,

their ten thousand sets of accountants, jobbers, and business dependents, with all they spent in advertising themselves and fighting one another, and the consumers must do the paying. What a famous process for beggaring a nation![3]

What Bellamy failed to see in this incredibly naive picture was that he was putting all the costs and inconveniences of "distribution" *on the buyer, on the consumer.* In his utopia it was the buyers who had to walk or take a trolley or drive their carriages to the "one great store." They could not go just around the corner to pick up groceries, or a loaf of bread or a bottle of milk; or a medicine; or a pad and pencil; or a screwdriver; or a pair of socks or stockings. No: for the most trivial item they had to walk or ride to the "one great store," no matter how far away it might happen to be. And then, because the one great nationalized store would not have any competition to meet, it would not put on enough salesmen, and the customers would have to queue up for indefinite waits (as in Russia or most government-run "services" anywhere). And, because of the same lack of competition, the goods would be poor and of limited variety. They would not be what the customers wanted, but what the government bureaucrats thought were plenty good enough for them.

The major error of Bellamy's picture lay in his complete failure to recognize the role of competition in constantly reducing costs of production, in improving products as well as means of production, and in developing wholly new products. He did not foresee the thousand inventions, improvements, and new discoveries that capitalistic competition has brought to the world in the seventy-six years since he wrote in 1888. Though he was supposed to be writing about conditions in the year 2000 (in his dream), he did not foresee the airplane or even the automobile; or radio or television or high-fidelity and stereophonic systems, or even the phonograph; or "automation," or a thousand miracles of the modern world. He did foresee music being piped into homes from central government stations by telephone; but this was because the telephone had already been *privately* invented by Alexander Graham Bell in 1876 and 1877 (ten years before Bellamy wrote), and had been privately improved since then.

Nor did he foresee the enormous economies that were to be effected in distribution. He did not foresee the enormous growth that was to develop in the size of the privately owned department store and in the varieties of goods it was to offer. He did not foresee that these stores would open branches in the suburbs or in other cities to serve their customers better. He did not foresee the development of the modern mail-order house, which would enable people to order goods from huge catalogs and save them the trouble of driving in to the "one great store" in the hope that it might carry what they wanted. He did not foresee the development of the modern supermarket, not only with its immense increase in the varieties of goods offered, but with its enormous economies in the size of sales staffs. And the reason he did not foresee these things is that he failed to recognize the enormous pressures that the competition which he deplored put on each individual store or firm constantly to increase its economies and reduce its costs.

And for the same reason he did not foresee the immense economies that were to be brought about by mechanized bookkeeping and accounting. In fact, his comments show that he hardly understood the need for bookkeeping or accounting at all. To him it was merely a way in which private merchants counted up their inexcusable profits. He knew nothing of one of the main functions of accounting. That a chief purpose of bookkeeping and accounting is precisely to know what costs are, and where they occur, so that wastes can be traced, pinpointed, and eliminated, and costs reduced, never occurred to him. He was against competition because he took all its beneficent results for granted.

I had not meant to get into economic considerations to this extent, but it seems necessary in order to show what is wrong with the implicit ethics of socialist or anti-capitalist writers.

3. "Equal Distribution" vs. Production

What socialist writers fail to understand is that only through the institution of the free market, with competition and private ownership of the means of production, and only through the interplay of prices, wages, costs, profits and losses is it possible to determine what consumers want, and in what relative proportions, and therefore what is to be produced, and in what relative proportions. Under a system of capitalism, the interplay of millions of prices and wages and trillions of price and wage and profit interrelationships produce the infinitely varied incentives and deterrents that direct production as by "an invisible hand" into thousands of different commodities and services. What socialists fail to understand is that socialism cannot solve the problem of "economic calculation." "Even angels, if they were endowed only with human reason, could not form a socialistic community."[4]

Now by any utilitarian standard (and the socialists themselves constantly appeal to a utilitarian standard) any system that cannot solve the problem of production, that cannot maximize production and cannot direct it into the proper channels, any system that would grossly reduce (compared with what is possible) the material basis for social life, the satisfaction of human wants, cannot be called a "moral" system.

We have already seen that a free-market system tends to give to every social group, and to every individual within each group, the value of what it or he has contributed to production. The working motto of such a system is: *To each what he creates.* Now Marxian socialism denies that capitalism tends to do this. It holds that under capitalism the worker is systematically "exploited" and robbed of the full produce of his labor. We have already seen in the preceding chapter that this Marxian contention is untenable.[5] But in any case the Marxists do not propose this for their own motto for distribution. Their motto is:

From each according to his ability; to each according to his need.

The two parts of this slogan are incompatible. Human nature is such that unless each is paid and rewarded according to his ability and effort and contribution he will not exert himself to apply and develop his full potential ability, to put forth his maximum effort, or to make his maximum contribution. And the general reduction of effort will of course reduce the production out of which everybody's needs are to be supplied. And that each will have "according to his need" is an empty boast—unless need is to be interpreted as meaning just enough to keep alive. (Even this, as the history of famines in Soviet Russia and Communist China has shown, is not always achieved.) But if "needs" are to be interpreted in the sense of wants and desires, in the sense of what each of us would like to have, it is a goal never to be fully achieved as long as there is an acknowledged shortage or scarcity of anything at all. If "need" is interpreted simply as *other people's* need as estimated by a Socialist bureaucrat, then no doubt the socialist goal can be sometimes achieved.

The most common ideal of "just" distribution espoused by utopian socialists is equal division of goods or income per head of the population.[6] Applied literally, this would violate the motto of distribution according to need by giving as much to infants as to adults in their prime. But the central objection to the ideal is of a quite different nature. It would destroy production.

We have already seen why this is so. Suppose at present (or at the time that the experiment of guaranteed equality of income per head is started) the statistical average income per capita is $2,500 per pay period. Then nobody who had been getting less than that would work harder to increase his income, because the difference would be guaranteed to him. In fact, as the whole amount would be guaranteed to him, he would see no reason to continue to work at all—except insofar as he was coerced into doing so by slavery, the whip, a tyrannical public opinion, or the intermittent and uncertain promptings of his own conscience. As, moreover, the new guaranteed *equality* of income at $2,500 per pay period could only be realized by seizing everything above that amount earned by anybody, those who had previously been earning more than that amount would no longer have any incentive to do so. In fact, they would no longer have any incentive to earn *even* that amount; because it would be guaranteed to them whether they earned it or not. The result would be general poverty and starvation.

It may be replied that this would be a suicidal thing for men to do, and that the inhabitants of such a society would surely be intelligent enough to see this; that they would be intelligent enough, in fact, to see that the more each produced the more there would be for all. This is in fact the argument of all socialists and of all socialist governments. What those who put forward the argument overlook is that what is true for the collectivity is not necessarily true for the individual. The individual is told by the managers of the socialist society that if he increases *his* output he will, other things being equal, increase *total* output. Mathematically he recognizes that this is so. But mathematically he recognizes, also, that under a system of *equal* division his own contribution can have only an infinitesimal relationship to his *own* income and welfare. He knows that even if he personally worked like a galley slave, and *nobody else* worked, he would still starve. And he knows, also, on the other hand, that if *everybody else* worked like a galley slave, and *he* did *nothing,* or only went through the motions of working when somebody was watching him, he would live very well on what *everybody else* had produced.

Suppose a man lives in a socialist country with a population of 200 million. By backbreaking work, say, he *doubles* his production. If his previous production was average, he has increased the total national production by only *one-two-hundred-millionth*. This means that he personally, assuming equal distribution, increases his income or consumption by only one-two-hundred-millionth, in spite of his terrific effort. He would never notice the infinitesimal difference in his material welfare. Suppose, on the other hand, that without getting caught he does not work at all. Then he gets only one-two-hundred-millionth less to eat. The deprivation is so infinitesimal that again he would be unable to notice it. But he would save himself from any work whatever.

In brief, under conditions of equal distribution regardless of individual production, a man's output, or the intensity of his effort, will be determined not by some abstract, overall, collectivist consideration but mainly by his assumption regarding what *everybody else* is doing or is going to do. He may be willing to "do his share"; but he'll be hanged before he'll break his back to produce while others are loafing, because he knows that it will get him nowhere. And he will probably be a little generous in measuring how hard he himself is working and a little cynical in estimating how hard everybody else is working. He will be apt to cite the very worst among his co-workers as typical of what "others" do while he slaves.[7]

That this is what actually happens in a completely socialized economy is proved by the necessity the managers of such an economy are under to maintain a constant propaganda in favor of *More Work, More Production.* It is proved by the mass starvation that immediately followed the collectivization of the farms in Soviet Russia and in Communist China. But no more impressive illustration can be found anywhere than in the very beginnings of American history.

Most of us have forgotten that when the Pilgrim Fathers landed on the shores of Massachusetts they established a communist system. Out of their common product and storehouse they set up a system of rationing, though it came to "but a quarter of a pound of bread a day to each person." Even when harvest came, "it arose to but a little." A vicious circle seemed to set in. The people complained that they were too weak from want of food to tend the crops as they should. Deeply religious though they were, they took to stealing from each other. "So as it well appeared," writes Governor Bradford, in his contemporary account, "that famine must still insue the next year allso, if not some way prevented."

So the colonists, he continues,

> begane to thinke how they might raise as much corne as they could, and obtaine a beter crope than they had done, that they might not still thus languish in miserie. At length [in 1623] after much debate of things, the Gov. (with the advise of the cheefest amongest them) gave way that they should set corne every man for his owne perticuler, and in that regard trust to them selves. . . . And so assigned to every family a parcell of land. . . .
>
> This had very good success; for it made all hands very industrious, so as much more corne was planted than other waise would have bene by any means the Gov. or any other could use, and saved him a great deall of trouble, and gave farr better contente.
>
> The women now wente willingly into the feild, and tooke their litle-ons with them to set corne, which before would aledg weakness, and inabilitie; whom to have compelled would have bene thought great tiranie and oppression.
>
> The experience that was had in this commone course and condition, tried sundrie years, and that amongst godly and sober men, may well evince the vanitie of that conceite of Platos and other ancients, applauded by some of later times;—that the taking away of propertie, and bringing in communitie into a comone wealth, would make them happy and flourishing; as if they were wiser than God. For this comunitie (so farr as it was) was found to breed much confusion and discontent, and retard much imployment that would have been to their benefite and comforte.
>
> For the yong-men that were most able and fitte for

labour and service did repine that they should spend their time and streingth to worke for other mens wives and children, with out any recompense. The strong, or man of parts, had no more in devission of victails and cloaths, than he that was weake and not able to doe a quarter the other could; this was thought injuestice. . . .

And for men's wives to be commanded to doe service for other men, as dressing their meate, washing their cloaths, etc., they deemd it a kind of slaverie, neither could many husbands well brooke it. . . .

By this time harvest was come, and instead of famine, now God gave them plentie, and the face of things was changed, to the rejoysing of the harts of many, for which they blessed God. And the effect of their particuler [private] planting was well seene, for all had, one way and other, pretty well to bring the year aboute, and some of the abler sorte and more industrious had to spare, and sell to others, so as any generall wante or famine hath not been amongest them since to this day.[8]

Such are the results when an attempt is made, in the name of "justice," to substitute a system of equal division per capita for a system of allowing each to get and keep what he creates. The fallacy of all schemes for (a *necessarily coercive*) equal division of wealth or income is that *they take production for granted.* The sponsors of such schemes tacitly assume that in spite of such equal division production will be the same; a few even explicitly argue that it will be greater.

4. Again: What Is Justice?

We must never lose sight of the fact that Justice, like Virtue, is primarily a means; and though it is also an end, it is never the ultimate end, but must be judged by its results. Whatever produces bad results, whatever reduces material welfare or human happiness, cannot be Justice. We call Justice the system of rules and arrangements that increase human peace, cooperation, production, and happiness, and Injustice whatever rules and arrangements stand in the way of these consequences. All *a priori* concepts of Justice must be revised accordingly.

The system of "to each what he produces," and the system of equal division regardless of what each produces, cannot, insofar as they are legal or governmental systems, be reconciled. It is commonly thought that while enforced equal division would be impracticable, precisely because it would discourage production, it is at least possible to mitigate the "injustices" and inequalities in wealth and income by various devices, the most popular of which in our day is the graduated income tax. The blessings of this tax in bringing about greatly increased "social justice" are constantly extolled. It is commonly assumed today, even by most academic economists, that personal incomes can be taxed up to 91 percent[9] without significantly reducing incentives or the capital accumulation upon which all improvement in economic conditions depends. It is just as commonly assumed that unemployment compensation and social security benefits can be increased or extended indefinitely without reducing the incentives to work and production. This is not the place to enter into a technical discussion of the economic effect of "progressive" income taxes and of welfare-state payments, or of a combination of the two. The reader may be referred for this to other sources.[10] Here it is sufficient to point out that whatever forced transfer of income from Peter to Paul reduces the total "social dividend" is a dubious gain for "justice."

So there was wisdom as well as wit in the old Victorian jingle:

What is a Communist?
A man who has yearnings,
For equal division
Of unequal earnings.

We are brought back once more to the question, What is the proper conception of Justice? A system under which the talented and skilled and industrious received no more than the incompetent and shiftless and lazy, and which equalized material rewards irrespective of effort, would certainly be unproductive; and to most of us, I think, it would also be unjust. Surely most of us would prefer, if we thought that were the only alternative, an enormously productive if not ideally "just" system to one which provided a perfectly "just" distribution of scarcity and poverty—"splendidly equalized destitution."[11] This does not mean that we prefer Abundance at the expense of Justice. It means that the term Just, as applied to material rewards, must be conceived as that system of distribution that tends in the long run to maximize everybody's incentives and so to maximize production and social cooperation.

There is one more principle of economic distribution, supported by some socialists, to be discussed. This is distribution or payment on the basis of "merit." This is a less naive principle than equal division per capita, and it is peculiarly likely to appeal to literary men, artists, poets, and intellectuals in other disciplines than economics. What a scandal, some of them say, that a vulgar and ill-mannered brewer or oil prospector, or the writer of a trashy novel, should make a fortune, while a fine modern poet almost starves because his volume sells only a few hundred copies or perhaps is not published at all. People should be rewarded in accordance with their true moral worth, or at least in accordance with their "real" contribution to our cultural life.

This proposed solution leaves the central question unanswered: Who is going to decide on people's true moral worth or "real" merit? Some of us may secretly believe that *we* would be competent to decide each person's true merits, and would reward them in proper proportion with absolute impartiality and justice, once we knew "the facts." But a little thought would convince most of us that only someone with the omniscience and impartiality of God would be able to decide on the relative merit and deserts of each of us. Where the solution is attempted in practice, as in Soviet Russia, we know the nightmarish results. The nearest approach to a practical answer has been the token solutions in contemporary England, with its annual awards of knighthoods and other titles, in France with election to the Academy, and in the United States with the distribution by its colleges of honorary degrees. But people have been known to question the justice or wisdom even of some of these.

5. Socialism Means Coercion

The solution of the free market is not perfect, but it is superior to any alternative that has been devised or seems likely to be devised. Under it material rewards correspond to the value that a man's particular services have to his fellows. The others reveal their valuations by what they are willing to pay for his contribution. The best-paid writers or manufacturers are those who offer the public what it wants, rather than what is good for it. What it wants will correspond with what is good for it only as the general level of taste and wisdom and morality rises. But whatever the defects of this system, any coercive or arbitrary substitute will surely be a great deal worse.

The central issue between capitalism and socialism is liberty: "It is of the essence of a free society that we should be materially rewarded not for doing what others order us to do, but for giving them what they want."[12] This does not mean that capitalism is more "materialistic" than socialism. "Free enterprise has developed the only kind of society which while it provides us with ample material means, if that is what we mainly want, still leaves the individual free to choose between material and non-material reward. . . . Surely it is unjust to blame a system as more materialistic because it leaves it to the individual to decide whether he prefers material gain to other kinds of excellence, instead of having this decided for him."[13]

What is not seen by those who are proposing other systems of material rewards than those provided by capitalism is that their systems can be imposed only by coercion. And coercion is the essence of socialism and communism. Under socialism there can be no free choice of occupation. Everyone must take the job to which he is assigned. He must go where he is sent. He must remain there until he gets orders to move elsewhere. His promotion or demotion depends upon the will of a superior, upon a single chain of command.

Economic life under socialism, in short, is organized on a military model. Each is assigned his task and platoon, as in an army. This is clear even in the utopian visions of a Bellamy: his people had to take their turns in the "army of labor," working in the mines, cleaning the streets, waiting on table—only, for some unexplained reason, all these tasks had suddenly become incomparably easier and more delightful. Engels assured his followers that: "Socialism will abolish both architecture and barrow-pushing as professions, and the man who has given half an hour to architecture will also push the cart a little until his work as an architect is again in demand. It would be a pretty sort of socialism which perpetuated the business of barrow- pushing."[14] In Bebel's Utopia only physical labor is recognized by society, and art and science are relegated to leisure hours.

What is implied but never clearly stated in these utopian visions is that everything will be done by coercion, by orders from the top. The press will be nationalized, intellectual life will be nationalized, freedom of speech will disappear.

The grim reality is shown today in the Russian slave camps and in Communist China. When economic liberty has been destroyed, all other liberty disappears with it. Alexander Hamilton recognized this clearly: "Power over a man's subsistence is power over his will." And as one of the masters of modern Russia—Leon Trotsky— pointed out even more clearly: "In a country where the sole employer is the State, opposition means death by slow starvation: The old principle: who does not work shall not eat, has been replaced by a new one: who does not obey shall not eat."

So complete socialism means the complete disappearance of

liberty. And, contrary to the Marxist propaganda of a century, it is socialism rather than capitalism that tends to lead to war. Capitalist countries have, it is true, gone to war with each other; but those who have been most strongly imbued with the philosophy of the free market and free trade have been the leaders of public opinion in opposition to war. Capitalism depends on the division of labor and on social cooperation. It therefore depends on the principle of peace, because the wider the field of social cooperation the greater the need for peace. The maximum of trade between nations (which all true liberals recognize to be mutually advantageous) requires the constant maintenance of peace. It was one of the first great liberals, David Hume, who wrote in his essay "Of the Jealousy of Trade" in 1740: "I shall therefore venture to acknowledge that, not only as a man, but as a British subject, I pray for the flourishing commerce of Germany, Spain, Italy, and even France itself. I am at least certain that Great Britain, and all those nations, would flourish more, did their sovereigns and their ministers adopt such enlarged and benevolent sentiments towards each other."

It is socialist governments, on the contrary, notwithstanding their denunciations of the Imperialist Warmongers, that blame their almost inevitable failures on the machinations of capitalist countries, and that have been the greatest source of modern wars. We need not rehearse here in detail the war record of the National Socialists in Germany (more popularly known today by their abbreviated name, the Nazis).[15] Nor need we rehearse the constant record of aggression, subversion, and conquest of Soviet Russia and Communist China—whether the conquest was only partly successful, as in Finland, South Korea, India, and Quemoy, or completely successful as in Lithuania, Latvia, Estonia, Czechoslovakia, Hungary, Rumania, Bulgaria, Albania, etc. We have in any case, as daily reminders, Khrushchev's constant threats to bury us.

6. A Religion of Immoralism

We are brought back, in fact, to the pervasive immorality of Marxism from its very beginnings to the present day. The noble end of socialism was thought to justify any means. As Max Eastman writes:

> Marx hated deity, and regarded high moral aspirations as an obstacle. The power on which he rested his faith in the coming paradise was the harsh, fierce, bloody evolution of a "material," and yet mysteriously "upward-going," world. And he convinced himself that, in order to get in step with such a world, we must set aside moral principles and go in for fratricidal war. Although buried under a mountain of economic rationalizations pretending to be science, that mystical and anti-moral faith is the one wholly original contribution of Karl Marx to man's heritage of ideas.[16]

Marx expelled people from his Communist party for mentioning programmatically such things as "love," "Justice," "humanity," even "morality" itself. When he founded the First International, he wrote privately to Engels: "I was obliged to insert in the preamble two phrases about 'duty and right,' ditto 'truth, morality, and justice'." But these lamentable phrases, he assured Engels, "are placed in such a way that they can do no harm."[17]

Lenin, a faithful follower, declared that in order to bring nearer the earthly socialist paradise: "We must be ready to employ trickery, deceit, law-breaking, withholding and concealing truth. We can and must write in a language which sows among the masses hate, revulsion, scorn, and the like, toward those who disagree with us."[18]

Addressing an all-Russian Congress of Youth, Lenin declared: "For us morality is subordinated completely to the interests of the class struggle of the proletariat."[19]

Stalin, when young, was an organizer of bank robberies and holdups. When he came into power he became one of the greatest mass murderers in history.

The motto of the Bolsheviks was simple: "Everything which promotes the success of the revolution is moral, everything which hinders it is immoral."

As Max Eastman exclaims, reviewing the record of this "religion of immoralism": "The notion of an earthly paradise in which men shall dwell together in millennial brotherhood is used to justify crimes and depravities surpassing anything the modern world has seen. . . . Such a disaster never happened to humanity before."[20]

---

1. See especially Ludwig von Mises's essay "Middle-of-the-Road Policy Leads to Socialism," in his *Planning for Freedom*. Also the essay by Gustav Cassel, *From Protectionism Through Planned Economy to Dictatorship* (London: Cobden-Sanderson, 1934).

2. For scores of specific examples, see Henry Hazlitt, *Economics in One Lesson.*

3. Edward Bellamy, *Looking Backward: 2000–1887,* 1888. Chap. 28. (Many editions.)

4. Ludwig von Mises, *Socialism,* p. 451.

5. And see Eugen Böhm-Bawerk, *Karl Marx and the Close of His System;* J. B. Clark, *The Distribution of Wealth;* and Ludwig von Mises, *Socialism.*

6. See the tremendously garrulous argument for this ideal in Bernard Shaw's *The Intelligent Woman's Guide to Socialism and Capitalism* (New York: Brentano's, 1928).

7. See Henry Hazlitt, *Time Will Run Back* (New Rochelle, N.Y.: Arlington House, 1966), pp. 88–93.

8. I related this history in an article in *Newsweek,* June 27, 1949.

9. The top U.S. rate until 1963.

10. See especially the chapters on Taxation and Social Security in F. A. Hayek's *The Constitution of Liberty.*

11. L. Garvin, *A Modern Introduction to Ethics,* p. 460.

12. F. A. Hayek, "The Moral Element in Free Enterprise," in *The Spiritual and Moral Significance of Free Enterprise,* p. 31.

13. *Ibid.,* pp. 31–32.

14. Quoted by Max Eastman, *Reflections on the Failure of Socialism* (New York: Devin-Adair, 1955), p. 83.

15. For that economic and war record, see Ludwig von Mises, *Omnipotent Government* (New Haven: Yale University Press, 1944).

16. Max Eastman, "The Religion of Immoralism," in *Reflections on the Failure of Socialism* (New York: Devin-Adair, 1955), Chap. 7, p. 83.

17. *Ibid.,* p. 85.

18. *Ibid.,* p. 87.

19. *Ibid.,* pp. 87–88.

20. *Ibid.,* p. 88.

CHAPTER 15

Morality and Religion

1. "If There's No God" —

Is religion necessary to the discovery of the specific moral rules that should guide us? And is a belief in the chief traditional doctrines of religion—such as the existence of a personal God, a life after death, a Heaven and a Hell—necessary in order to secure human observance of moral rules?

The belief that morality is impossible without religion has dominated the thought of the Western world for nearly twenty centuries. In its crudest form, it is put into the mouth of Smerdyakov Karamazov, in the terrible scene in which he confesses to his half-brother Ivan, a philosophical atheist, that he has murdered and robbed their father: "I was only your instrument," says Smerdyakov, "your faithful servant, and it was following your words I did it. . . . 'All things are lawful.' That was quite right what you taught me. . . . For if there's no everlasting God, there's no such thing as virtue, and there's no need of it."[1]

And Santayana satirizes the same type of argument: "It is a curious assumption of religious moralists that their precepts would never be adopted unless people were persuaded by external evidence that God had positively established them. Were it not for divine injunction and threats everyone would like nothing better than to kill and to steal and to bear false witness." [2]

2. The Indictment

Perhaps we can best arrive at an answer to the two questions that led off this chapter by reviewing the principal arguments on both sides.

Let us begin with the argument of those who have denied that religious faith is necessary for the maintenance of morality. Perhaps the fullest statement of this is that made by John Stuart Mill in his essay on "The Utility of Religion."[3] Mill begins by contending that religion has always received excessive credit for maintaining morality because, whenever morality is formally taught, especially to children, it is almost invariably taught as religion. Children are not taught to distinguish between the commands of God and the commands of their parents. The major motive to morality, Mill argues, is the good opinion of our fellows. The threat of punishment for our sins in a Hereafter exercises only a dubious and uncertain force: "Even the worst malefactor is hardly able to think that any crime he has had it in his power to commit, any evil he can have inflicted in this short space of existence, can have deserved torture extending through an eternity." In any case, "the value of religion as a supplement to human laws, a more cunning sort of police, an auxiliary to the thief-catcher and the hangman, is not that part of its claims which the more high-minded of its votaries are fondest of insisting on."

There is a real evil, too, in ascribing a supernatural origin to the received maxims of morality. "That origin consecrates the whole of them, and protects them from being discussed or criticized." The result is that the morality becomes "stereotyped"; it is not improved and perfected, and dubious precepts are preserved along with the noblest and most necessary.

Even the morality that men have achieved through the fear or the love of God, Mill maintains, can also be achieved by those of us who seek, not only the approbation of those whom we respect, but the imagined approbation of

all those, dead or living, whom we admire or venerate. . . . The thought that our dead parents or friends would have approved our conduct is a scarcely less powerful motive than the knowledge that our living ones do approve it: and the idea that Socrates, or [John] Howard, or Washington, or Antoninus, or Christ, would have sympathized with us, or that we are attempting to do our part in the spirit in which they did theirs, has operated on the very best minds, as a strong incentive to act up to their highest feelings and convictions.

On the other hand,

the religions which deal in promises and threats regarding a future life . . . fasten down the thoughts to the person's own posthumous interests; they tempt him to regard the performance of his duties to others mainly as a means to his own personal salvation; and are one of the most serious obstacles to the great purpose of moral culture, the strengthening of the unselfish and weakening of the selfish element in our nature. . . . The habit of expecting to be rewarded in another life for our conduct in this, makes even virtue itself no longer an exercise of the unselfish feelings.

Mill makes further remarks regarding what he considers the elements of positive immorality in the Judean and Christian religions, but an even more bitter and unqualified indictment is made by philosopher Morris R. Cohen:

The absolute character of religious morality has made it emphasize the sanctions of fear—the terrifying consequences of disobedience. I do not wish to ignore the fact that the greatest religious teachers have laid more stress on the love of the good for its own sake. But in the latter respect they have not been different from such great philosophers as Democritus, Aristotle, or Spinoza, who regarded morality as its own reward.

Religion has made a virtue of cruelty. Bloody sacrifices

of human beings to appease the gods fill the pages of history. In ancient Mexico we have the wholesale sacrifice of prisoners of war as a form of national cultus. In the ancient East we have the sacrifice of children to Moloch. Even the Greeks were not entirely free from this religious custom. Let us note that while the Old Testament prohibits the ancient Oriental sacrifice of the first-born, it does not deny its efficacy in the case of the King of Moab (II Kings 3:2) nor is there, any revulsion at the readiness with which Abraham was willing to sacrifice his son Isaac. In India it was the religious duty of the widow to be burned on the funeral pyre of her late husband. And while Christianity formally condemned human sacrifice, it revived it in fact under the guise of burning heretics. I pass over the many thousands burned by order of the Inquisition, and the record of the hundreds of people burned by rulers like Queen Mary for not believing in the Pope or in transubstantiation. The Protestant Calvin burned the scholarly Servetus for holding that Jesus was "the son of the eternal God" rather than "the eternal son of God." And in our own Colonial America heresy was a capital offense.

Cruelty is a much more integral part of religion than most people nowadays realize. The Mosaic law commands the Israelites, whenever attacking a city, to kill all the males, and all females who have known men. The religious force of this is shown when Saul is cursed and his whole dynasty is destroyed for leaving one prisoner, King Agag, alive. Consider that tender psalm, "By the rivers of Babylon." After voicing the pathetic cry "How can we sing the songs of Jehovah in a foreign land?" it goes on to curse Edom, and ends "Happy shall he be, that taketh and dasheth thy little ones against the rock." Has there been any religious movement to expurgate this from the religious service of Jews and Christians? Something of the spirit of this intense hatred for the enemies of God (i.e., those not of our own religion) has invented and developed the terrors of Hell, and condemned almost all of mankind to suffer them eternally—all, that is, except a few members of our own particular religion. Worst of all, it has regarded these torments as adding to the beatitude of the saints. The doctrine of a loving and all-merciful God professed by Christianity or Islam has not prevented either one from preaching and practicing the duty to hate and persecute those who do not believe. Nay, it has not prevented fierce wars between diverse sects of these religions, such as the wars between Shiites, Sunnites, and Wahabites, between Greek Orthodox, Roman Catholics, and Protestants.

The fierce spirit of war and hatred is not, of course, entirely due to religion. But religion *has* made a *duty* of hatred. It preached crusades against Mohammedans and forgave atrocious sins to encourage indiscriminate slaughter of Greek Orthodox as well as of Mohammedan populations.

Cruel persecution and intolerance are not accidents, but grow out of the very essence of religion, namely, its absolute claims. So long as each religion claims to have absolute, supernaturally revealed truth, all other religions are sinful errors. . . . There is no drearier chapter in the history of human misery than the unusually bloody internecine religious or sectarian wars which have drenched in blood so much of Europe, Northern Africa, and Western Asia. . . .

The complacent assumption which identifies religion with higher morality ignores the historic fact that there is not a single loathsome human practice that has not at some time or other been regarded as a religious duty. I have already mentioned the breaking of promises to heretics. But assassination and thuggery (as the words themselves indicate), sacred prostitution (in Babylonia and India), diverse forms of self-torture, and the verminous uncleanliness of saints like Thomas à Becket, have all been part of religion. The religious conception of morality has been a legalistic one. Moral rules are the commands of the gods. But the latter are sovereigns and not themselves subject to the rules which they lay down for others according to their own sweet wills.[4]

3. The Defense

In the face of such sweeping indictments, what have the defenders of religion as an indispensable basis of morality had to say? Rather strangely, it is not easy to find among recent writers on ethics uncompromising and powerful exponents of this traditional view. If we turn, for example, to the Reverend Hastings Rashdall, where we might expect to find such a view, we are surprised at the modesty of his claims. His ideas are presented at length in his well-known two-volume work, *The Theory of Good and Evil* (1907), in the two chapters on "Metaphysics and Morality" and "Religion and Morality." But in a little volume of less than a hundred pages, written a few years later, which he describes in a preface as "necessarily little more than a condensation of my Theory of Good and Evil, he has himself formally summarized his views on the subject. It seems to me best to quote his own summary almost in full:

1. Morality cannot be based upon or deduced from any metaphysical or theological proposition whatever. The moral judgment is ultimate and immediate. Putting this into more popular language, the immediate recognition that I ought to act in a certain way supplies a sufficient reason for so acting entirely apart from anything else that I may believe about the ultimate nature of things.

2. But the recognition of the validity of Moral Obligation in general or of any particular moral judgment logi-

cally implies the belief in a permanent spiritual self which is really the cause of its own actions. Such a belief is in the strictest sense a postulate of Morality.

3. The belief in God is not a postulate of Morality in such a sense that the rejection of it involves a denial of all meaning or validity to our moral judgments, but the acceptance or rejection of this belief does materially affect the sense which we give to the idea of obligation. The belief in the objectivity of moral judgments implies that the moral law is recognized as no merely accidental element in the construction of the human mind, but as an ultimate fact about the Universe. This rational demand cannot be met by any merely materialistic or naturalistic Metaphysic, and is best satisfied by a theory which explains the world as an expression of an intrinsically righteous rational Will, and the moral consciousness as imperfect revelation of the ideal towards which that will is directed. The belief in God may be described as a postulate of Morality in a less strict or secondary sense.

4. So far from Ethics being based upon or deduced from Theology, a rational Theology is largely based upon Ethics: since the moral Consciousness supplies us with all the knowledge we possess as to the action, character, and direction of the supreme Will, and forms an important element in the argument for the existence of such a Will.

5. We must peremptorily reject the view that the obligation of Morality depends upon sanctions, i.e., reward and punishment, in this life or any other. But, as the belief in an objective moral law naturally leads up to and requires for its full justification the idea of God, so the idea of God involves the belief in Immortality if the present life seems an inadequate fulfillment of the moral ideal. In ways which need not be recapitulated, we have seen that it is practically

a belief eminently favorable to the maximum influence of the moral ideal on life.

The whole position may perhaps be still more simply summed up. It is possible for a man to know his duty, and to achieve considerable success in doing it, without any belief in God or Immortality or any of the other beliefs commonly spoken of as religious; but he is likely to know and do it better if he accepts a view of the Universe which includes as its most fundamental articles these two beliefs.[5]

4. Ethics of the Old Testament

After this brief glance at some of the conflicting arguments, what should our own answer be to the two questions with which this chapter began? Let us begin with the first.

It is hard to see how religious beliefs by themselves can give any guidance to the specific moral rules that should guide us. We are brought back to the old theologic problem: Religion tells us that we ought to act in accordance with the will of God. But is an action right simply because God wills it? Or does God will it because it is right? We cannot conceive of God's arbitrarily commanding us to do anything but the Right, or forbidding us to do anything but the Wrong. Are actions moral because God wills them, or does God will them because they are moral? Which, logically or temporally, comes first: God's will, or morality?

There is a further theologic problem. If God is omnipotent, how can His will fail to be realized, whether we do right or wrong?

Then there is the practical ethical problem. Assuming that it is our duty to follow God's will, how can we know what God does will, either in general or in any particular case? Who is privy to God's will? Who is presumptuous enough to assume that he knows the will of God? How do we determine God's will? By intuition? By special revelation? By reason? In the latter case, are we to assume that God desires the happiness of men? Then we are brought back to the position of utilitarianism. Are we to assume that He desires the "perfection" of men, or their "self- realization," or that they live "according to nature"? Then we are brought back to one of these traditional ethical philosophies—but purely by our own assumptions, and not by direct or unmistakable knowledge of God's will.

A hundred different religions give a hundred different accounts or interpretations of God's will in the moral realm. Most Christians assume that it is found in the Bible. But when we turn to the Bible we find hundreds of moral commandments, laws, judgments, injunctions, teachings, precepts. Often these preachments flatly contradict each other. How are we to reconcile the Mosaic "Eye for eye, tooth for tooth, hand for hand, foot for foot, Burning for burning, wound for wound, stripe for stripe"[6] with the direct contradiction of it in Christ's Sermon on the Mount: "Ye have heard that it hath been said, An eye for an eye, and a tooth for a tooth: But I say unto you, That ye resist not evil: but whosoever shall smite thee on thy right cheek, turn to him the other also. . . .

"Ye have heard that it hath been said, Thou shalt love thy neighbor, and hate thine enemy. But I say unto you, Love your enemies, bless them that curse you, do good to them that hate you and pray for them which despitefully use you, and persecute you."[7]

Broadly speaking, the ethical precepts of the Old and New Testaments are not only in contradiction with each other in detail, but even in their general spirit. The Old Testament commands obedience to God through fear; the New Testament pleads for obedience to God through love.

Some people are fond of saying, unthinkingly, that all the moral guidance we need is to be found in the Ten Commandments. They forget that the Ten Commandments are not specifically limited to ten in the Bible itself, but are immediately followed by more than a hundred other commandments (called, however, "judgments").

They forget also that Christ himself insisted on the need for supplementing them. "A new commandment I give unto you, That ye love one another."[8] And Jesus put more emphasis on this commandment, in his life and in his teachings, than on any other.

When we take the Ten Commandments simply by themselves, we find that, if it were not for their supposed sacred origin, we would regard them as a rather strange and unbalanced assortment of moral rules. Working on the Sabbath day, if we judge by the relative emphasis given to it (94 words), is regarded as a much more serious sin or crime than committing murder (four words). Nor is there any indication, for that matter, that adultery, stealing, or bearing false witness is any less serious a sin or crime than murder. It is apparently no greater sin to steal something than merely to covet it; and the reason it is a sin to covet your neighbor's wife is apparently because she is, like his house, his manservant, his maidservant, his ox or his ass, part of your neighbor's property. Finally, the God of the Ten Commandments is not only, by His own confession, "a jealous God," but an incredibly vindictive one, "visiting the iniquity of the fathers upon the children unto the third and fourth generation of them that hate me."

Immediately following the Ten Commandments God ordered Moses to set before the children of Israel more than a hundred judgments or laws. The first one orders that if anyone buy a Hebrew slave, the slave shall serve six years and be set free in the seventh. Whoever strikes a man so that he dies is to be put to death—but so is whoever curses his father or mother. And "Thou shalt not suffer a witch to live."[9]

But enough has already been said here (and in the quotation in this chapter from Morris R. Cohen) to establish without further evidence at least the negative conclusion that the ethics of the Old Testament, explicit and implied, are not a reliable guide to conduct for twentieth-century man.[10]

5. Ethics of the New Testament

In the New Testament we find a strikingly different ethic. In place of the God of vengeance, to be feared, we find the God of Mercy, to be loved. The new commandment, "that ye love one another," and the example of the personal life and preaching of Jesus of Nazareth, have had a more profound influence on our moral aspirations and ideals than any other rule or Person in history.

But the ethical doctrines of Jesus present serious difficulties. We can, in large part, command our actions; but we cannot command our feelings. We cannot love all our fellow men simply because we think we ought to. Love for a few (usually members of our immediate family), affection and friendship for some, initial goodwill toward a wider circle, and the attempt constantly to discourage and suppress within ourselves incipient anger, resentment, jealousy, envy, or hatred, are the most that all but a very small number of us seem able to achieve. We may give lip-service to turning the other cheek, to loving our enemies, blessing those that curse us, doing good to those that hate us, but we cannot bring ourselves, except on the rarest occasions, to take these injunctions literally. (I am speaking here not of our duty to be just, or even outwardly kind, toward all, but of our ability to *command our inner feelings* toward all.)

Notwithstanding Matthew 7:1, "Judge not, that ye be not judged," all modern nations have policemen, courts, and judges. Most of us, whether or not we occasionally consider the beam in our own eye, cannot refrain from pointing out the mote in our brother's eye. The overwhelming majority of us are no more capable than the rich young man who came to Jesus (Matthew 19:20–22) of trying to be perfect by selling all that we have and giving the proceeds to the poor. Though it is all but impossible for a rich man to enter the kingdom of heaven (Matthew 19:24–25) most of us try to become as rich as we can and hope for the best hereafter. In spite of Matthew 6:25–28, we do take thought of our life, what we shall eat, what we shall drink, and wherewithal we shall be clothed. We do sow and reap and gather into barns, we do work and save, we do take care of ourselves in the hope of adding to our span of life.

The problem is not merely that we are incapable of reaching moral perfection. That we cannot achieve perfection is no reason why we should not set our conception of it before us as a shining ideal. The question goes deeper than this. Are some of the ideals of Jesus' teaching practicable? Would the life of the individual, or would the lives of the mass of mankind, be more satisfactory or less satisfactory if we tried literally to follow some of these precepts?

The morality taught by Jesus was apparently based on the assumption that "the time is fulfilled, and the kingdom of God is at hand: repent ye, and believe the gospel."[11]

> Jesus regards himself as the prophet of the approaching Kingdom of God, the Kingdom which according to ancient prophecy shall bring redemption from all earthly insufficiency, and with it all economic cares. His followers have nothing to do but to prepare themselves for this Day. The time for worrying about earthly matters is past, for now, in expectation of the Kingdom, men must attend to more important things. Jesus offers no rules for earthly action and struggle; his Kingdom is not of this world. Such rules of conduct as he gives his followers are valid only for the short interval of time which has still to be lived while waiting for the great things to come. In the Kingdom of God there will be no economic cares.[12]

Whether this interpretation is correct or not, practically all but the earliest Christians abandoned this notion and the "transitional" morality based upon it. As Santayana has put it: "If a religious morality is to become that of society at large—which original Christian morality was never meant to be—it must adapt its maxims to a possible system of worldly economy."[13]

6. Conclusion

We must come, then, to this conclusion. Ethics is autonomous. It is not dependent upon any specific religious doctrine. And the great body of ethical rules, even those laid down by the Fathers of the Church, have no necessary connection with any religious premises. We need merely point, in illustration, to the great ethical system of Thomas Aquinas. As Henry Sidgwick tells us,

> The moral philosophy of Thomas Aquinas is, in the main, Aristotelianism with a Neo-Platonic tinge, interpreted and supplemented by a view of Christian doctrine derived chiefly from Augustine. . . . When . . . among moral virtues he distinguishes Justice, manifested in actions by which others receive their due, from the virtues that primarily relate to the passions of the agent himself, he is giving his interpretation of Aristotle's doctrine; and his list of the latter virtues, to the number of ten, is taken *en bloc* from the Nicomachean Ethics.[14]

This great similarity in the ethical code of persons of profound differences in religious belief should not be surprising. In human history religion and morality are like two streams that sometimes run parallel, sometimes merge, sometimes separate, sometimes seem independent and sometimes interdependent. But morality is older than any living religion and probably older than all religion. We find a kind of moral code—or at least what, if we found it in human beings, we would call moral behavior—even among the lower animals.[15]

Let us return now to the second question with which this chapter opened. Even if religion cannot tell us anything about what the specific moral rules ought to be, is it necessary in order to secure observance of the moral code? The best answer we can make, I think, is that while religious faith is not indispensable to such observance, it must be recognized in the present state of civilization as a powerful force in securing the observance that exists. I am not speaking primarily of the effect of a belief in a future life, in a Heaven or a Hell, though this is by no means unimportant. Doing good deeds in the hope of reward in a future life, or refraining from evil in the fear of punishment in such a future life, has been shrewdly called religious utilitarianism; but though the motive is purely self-regarding, the result may be so far beneficent, like the result of what Bentham calls extra-regarding prudence.

The most powerful religious belief supporting morality, however, seems to me of a much different nature. This is the belief in a God who sees and knows our every action, our every impulse and our every thought, who judges us with exact justice, and who, whether or not He rewards us for our good deeds and punishes us for our evil ones, approves of our good deeds and disapproves of our evil ones. Perhaps, as Mill suggests, for this conception of God as the all-seeing and all-judging Witness there can be effectively substituted, as there is in many agnostics, an almost equally effective thought of what our parents or friends, or some great human figure, living or dead, whom we deeply admire or revere, would think of our action or secret thought if they or he knew of it. Still, the belief in an all-knowing and all-judging God remains a tremendous force in ethical conduct today.

There is no doubt that decay of religious faith tends to let loose license and immorality. This is what has been happening in our own generation. Yet it is not the function of the moral philosopher, as such, to proclaim the truth of this religious faith or to try to maintain it. His function is, rather, to insist on the rational basis of all morality, to point out that it does not need any supernatural assumptions, and to show that the rules of morality are or ought to be those rules of conduct that tend most to increase human cooperation, happiness and well-being in this our present life.[16]

---

1. Fyodor Dostoyevsky, *The Brothers Karamazov* (1880), Part III, Book XI, Chap. VIII.

2. George Santayana, *Dominations and Powers*, p. 156.

3. John Stuart Mill, *Three Essays on Religion* (1874), p. 3.

4. Morris R. Cohen, "The Dark Side of Religion," in *The Faith of a Liberal* (New York: Henry Holt, 1946), pp. 348–352.

5. Hastings Rashdall, *Ethics* (London: T. C. & E. C. Jack), pp. 92–93.

6. Exodus 21:24–25.

7. Matthew 5:38–39, 43–44.

8. John 13:34.

9. Exodus 21:2, 12, 17; 22:18.

10. We must remember, however, that the injunction to "love thy neighbor as thyself" occurs in the Old Testament (Leviticus 19:18) as well as in the New (Luke 10:27).

11. Mark 1:15.

12. The quotation is from Ludwig von Mises, *Socialism,* pp. 413-414, but Mises is merely summarizing the views of such theologians as Harnack, Giessen, and Troeltsch.

13. George Santayana, *Dominations and Powers,* p. 157.

14. Henry Sidgwick, *Outlines of the History of Ethics* (1886) (London: Macmillan, 1949), pp. 141–142.

15. I refer the reader to many passages in the works of Charles Darwin, Herbert Spencer, E. P. Thompson, G. J. Romanes, Prince Kropotkin, C. Lloyd Morgan, W. L. Lindsay, E. L. Thorndike, Albert Schweitzer, R. M.Yerkes, H. Eliot Howard, W. C. Allee, F. Alverdes, Wolfgang Köhler, Konrad C. Lorenz, Julian Huxley, W. T. Hornaday, David Katz, C. R. Carpenter, William Morton Wheeler, and Joy Adamson. I believe that morality has at least a partly innate and instinctual basis, and that this has developed because of its survival value, both for the individual and for the species. I consider this, however, primarily a biological rather than an ethical problem, and I shall not discuss it here.

16. This conclusion, I am happy to find, does not differ essentially from that of Stephen Toulmin: "Where there is a good moral reason for choosing one course of action rather than another, morality is not to be contradicted by religion. Ethics provides the *reasons* for choosing the 'right' course; religion helps us to put our *hearts* into it." *An Examination of the Place of Reason in Ethics*, p. 219. The case is even more compactly summed up by William James: "Whether a God exist, or whether no God exist, in yon blue heaven above us bent, we form at any rate an ethical republic here below." "The Moral Philosopher and the Moral Life" (1891), in *Pragmatism and Other Essays* (Washington Square Press Book, 1963), p. 223.

Biographical Notes

(Prepared by Bettina Bien Greaves)

Thomas Aquinas (Saint) (1224?-1274), Italian scholastic philosopher.

Bebel, August (1840–1913), German Socialist Democratic leader, author of *Women and Socialism* (1910).

Bellamy, Edward (1850–1898), American utopian socialist and author of *Looking Backward* (1888).

Blackstone, Sir William (1723–1780), English jurist and author of *Commentaries on the Laws of England.*

Burke, Edmund (1739–1797), British statesman and orator who sided with the American colonies during our Revolution; an ardent opponent of the Jacobin radicalism of the French Revolution.

Butler, Joseph (1692–1752), British theologian and bishop.

Clark, John Bates (1847–1938), American economist who explained that the market tends to distribute wealth to each individual according to his/her respective contribution; professor at Columbia University (1895–1923).

Cohen, Morris R. (1880–1947), Russian-born American philosopher and educator.

Confucius (551–479 B.C.), Chinese philosopher whose precepts dealt with morals, family, social reform, and statecraft.

Eastman, Max F. (1883–1969), American Communist fellow-traveler who lived to reject Marx's immorality and become an advocate of free markets.

Engels, Friedrich (1820–1895), lifetime associate and supporter of Karl Marx; collaborated with Marx in writing the *Communist Manifesto* (1847).

Fitzgerald, F. Scott (1896–1940), American writer of fiction.

France, Anatole (1844–1924), French novelist, critic, playwright, and satirist.

Grotius, Hugo (1583–1645), Dutch jurist and statesman who developed the basis for "international law."

Hayek, Friedrich A. von (1899–1992), Austrian-school economist and political philosopher; winner of Nobel Prize in economics in 1974.

Hobbes, Thomas (1588–1679), English moral philosopher who, according to Hazlitt, held "that people are guided only by egoistic motives."

Holmes, Oliver Wendell, Jr. (1841–1935), American jurist and Associate Justice on the U.S. Supreme Court (1902–1932).

Hume, David (1711–1776), Scottish philosopher and historian who held that morality depends on aspects of human nature such as self-interest and altruistic sympathy; Hazlitt considered Hume to be "probably the greatest of British philosophers."

Huxley, Thomas Henry (1825–1895), British biologist, an agnostic, who believed we could not know anything beyond our senses, and a principal exponent of Darwinian evolution.

James, William (1842–1910), American psychologist and philosopher; one of the founders of the philosophy of pragmatism.

Kant, Immanuel (1724–1804), German metaphysician and transcendental philosopher; founder of critical philosophy.

Keynes, John Maynard (1883–1946), English economist who recommended politically popular, short-run inflationist government spending programs in order to solve economic problems.

Khrushchev, Nikita S. (1894–1971), Soviet leader and premier of the U.S.S.R. (1958–1964).

Locke, John (1632–1704), English political philosopher whose ideas on government influenced the authors of the American Declaration of Independence and Constitution.

Marx, Karl (1818–1883), German-born founder of Communism and advocate of the revolution of the workers against their capitalist exploiters. Author of *The Communist Manifesto* and *Das Kapital.*

Mill, John Stuart (1806–1873), English economist and advocate of utilitarianism.

Nietzsche, Friedrich Wilhelm (1844–1900), German philosopher; his theory of the "superman" and a "master morality" influenced a number of Nazi officials.

Nock, Albert Jay (1870–1945), American writer, individualist, and independent thinker.

Pound, Roscoe (1870–1964), American educator and lawyer; Dean of the Harvard Law School (1916–1936).

Rashdall, Hastings (1858–1924), British moral philosopher, theologian, and historian of universities.

Rousseau, Jean Jacques (1712–1778), French philosopher and author, held political theory rested on "general will."

Santayana, George (1863–1952), Spanish-born American poet and philosopher; as a philosopher he sought to understand pleasure and value.

Sidgwick, Henry (1838–1900), English philosopher and follower of John Stuart Mill; blended utilitarianism with intuition, prudence, benevolence, and justice.

Smith, Adam (1723–1790), Scottish economist who is considered the founder of "classical" economics; author of the world-renowned *Wealth of Nations* (1776).

Spencer, Herbert (1820–1903), English philosopher, an individualist; his wide-ranging works dealt with morality, freedom, and government.

Stalin, Joseph (1879–1953), Russian Communist dictator of U.S.S.R. (1924–1953).

Trotsky, Leon (1879–1940), Russian Communist, after Lenin's death became a rival of Stalin's; forced to flee, he went to Mexico where he was murdered.

Wicksteed, Philip (1844–1927), English Unitarian minister and economist whose "great contribution," according to Hazlitt, "was to dispose of the persistent idea that economic activity is exclusively egoistic or self-regarding."

Bibliographical Essay

Henry Hazlitt read widely and was a true scholar. After he decided to write on morality, it was natural, as he wrote in the Preface to the unabridged version of this book, that he should begin "to think and read more about the problems of ethics." Because this field had been so thoroughly explored by previous writers, he felt it would appear "haphazard and arbitrary" to make specific acknowledgments. However, he cited and quoted from the works of many authors whose reasoning and ideas he discussed. There is little point in listing, with bibliographical information, all the books he mentioned; readers looking for particular titles should find enough information in the Endnotes to identify them and locate them through their library. As a matter of fact, many of the books, have been reprinted, some many times over, and are still in print. However, some titles are worthy of special mention.

Hazlitt "learned most," he said, from the British Utilitarians, beginning with the well-known philosopher, David Hume, and running through Adam Smith, Jeremy Bentham, John Stuart Mill, and Henry Sidgwick. He mentioned specifically Hume's *Inquiry Concerning the Principles of Morals* (1752), reissued in 1975 by Oxford University Press, and *A Treatise of Human Nature,* which has been reprinted many times. Adam Smith's *Wealth of Nations* (1776) is a classic; the standard edition for many years, edited and indexed by Edwin Cannan, was published by Modern Library/Random House (1937), and more recently (1977) by University of Chicago Press. A deluxe edition of Smith's *The Theory of Moral Sentiments* (1759) was issued in 1987 by Liberty Fund of Indianapolis. John Stuart Mill's *Utilitarianism* (1861) and his *Three Essays on Religion* (1874) have both been reprinted. Although Hazlitt thought well of Jeremy Bentham and referred to him many times, Bentham has not retained the popularity of Smith or Mill and his books that Hazlitt referred to, *Deontology* and *Morals and Legislation,* are apparently out of print. Henry Sidgwick's *Methods of Ethics* and *Outlines of the History of Ethics* (1886) are both available in recent editions.

Hazlitt held that modern economics had "worked out answers to the problems of individual and social value . . . which. . . . throw great light on some of the central problems of ethics" so he quoted from the works of many economists, most notably the Austrian economists. He maintained that his "greatest indebtedness" was to the Austrian, Ludwig von Mises. As a matter of fact Hazlitt said that he was led in part to write this book because he thought Mises's ethical observations, which appeared only as "brief incidental passages in his great contributions to economics and 'praxeology'," should be further developed.

Hazlitt cites several books by Mises, including his major economic treatise, *Human Action* (1st edition, 1949). The 3rd edition (1966) is now available in paperback. A 4th edition, hardcovered, with a new index was issued by the Foundation for Economic Education (FEE) in 1996. Also mentioned here is Mises's *Socialism,* published originally in German in 1922, translated into English in 1932 and published in this country in 1952 by Yale University Press, has been kept in print almost continuously. The latest edition, put out by Liberty Fund of Indianapolis, is still available. Mises's *Theory and History* (Yale, 1957) was reprinted in 1985 by the Ludwig von Mises Institute of Auburn, Alabama. His *Liberalism,* first published in German in 1927 and translated into English in 1962, was out of print for many years but a fourth edition of the English version appeared under the aegis of FEE in 1995. Several editions of *Planning for Freedom* (1952), an anthology of Mises's papers and addresses, have been published, the latest by Libertarian Press, now of Grove City, Pennsylvania.

Hazlitt quotes also from the writings of other Austrian economists—notably Eugen von Böhm-Bawerk and F. A. Hayek. Böhm-Bawerk's major work was the three-volume *Capital and Interest*

(English translation, 1959). In this book, Hazlitt cites Böhm-Bawerk's monograph, "Karl Marx and the Close of his System" (1896), reprinted in 1975 by the New York publisher, Augustus M. Kelley. It is still available under a different title, "Unresolved Contradiction in the Marxian Economic System," in *Shorter Classics of Böhm-Bawerk* (Libertarian Press, 1962).

Hazlitt refers to Austrian F. A. Hayek's *The Constitution of Liberty* (University of Chicago Press, 1960), which the Press has kept in print since Hayek won the Nobel prize for economics in 1974. Hayek's 1961 essay mentioned here, "The Moral Element in Free Enterprise," is included in *The Morality of Capitalism* (FEE, 2nd edition 1996), in the Hayek anthology, *Studies in Philosophy, Politics and Economics* (University of Chicago Press, 1967) and in the multi-volume edition of Hayek's *Collected Works* now being published by the University of Chicago Press.

As the reader of this book will see, Hazlitt thought highly of the Englishman Philip Wicksteed, crediting him with having disposed of "the persistent idea that economic activity is exclusively egoistic or self-regarding." Wicksteed's 2-volume *The Common Sense of Political Economy* (1910), was reprinted in 1933 by Routledge & Keagan Paul of London and in 1950 by Augustus M. Kelley, but is apparently no longer in print.

Hazlitt refers also to the works of American economists. John Bates Clark's *The Distribution of Wealth* (1899) was reprinted in 1965 by Augustus M. Kelley. Israel M. Kirzner's *The Economic Point of View* (1960) is no longer in print, although many of Kirzner's more recent publications on capital, competition and entrepreneurship are. *Man, Economy and State* by Murray N. Rothbard (2 volumes, Van Nostrand, 1962) has been published as a massive paperback and was reprinted (1993) by the Ludwig von Mises Institute of Auburn, Alabama.

Among the other notable authors Hazlitt cites is the English political philosopher, John Locke. In the 1680s when John Locke was working on *A Second Treatise of Civil Government,* his ideas on parliamentary government and the separation of powers were considered dangerous and he thought it wise to leave England. In 1683, he went to Holland, returning only in 1689 after the Stuart king James II had been deposed and William and Mary brought in as rulers. Locke's *Treatise* was published in 1690.

Many publishers, including Liberty Fund of Indianapolis (1988), have put out editions of Bernard de Mandeville's *The Fable of the Bees* (1729). In that book Mandeville compared a beehive, with its division of labor, with the economy; according to him even "private vices" are "publick benefits" for prosperity also results when producers satisfy the demands of the greedy, envious, and avaricious.

Hazlitt wrote in the Preface to the unabridged edition of this book, that his chief sources for the relations between law and ethics were, Paul Vinogradoff, Roscoe Pound, and F. A. Hayek. Vinogradoff's *Common-Sense in Law* (Henry Holt, 1914) was reprinted in 1975 by Ayer; Pound's *Law and Morals* (University of North Carolina Press, 1926) was reprinted in 1987 by Rothman. Although not published until after the appearance of Hazlitt's *Foundations of Morality* (1964), Hayek's three volumes—*Law, Legislation and Liberty* (1973, 1976, and 1979)— published by the University of Chicago Press as were Hayek's other works mentioned above, would also be pertinent.

Hazlitt refers several times to his own popular *Economics in One Lesson* (1st ed., Harper, 1946), often reprinted and now a Crown publication. A special 50th anniversary edition was issued in 1996 by Laissez Faire Books. This book is available, as it has been ever since its original publication, from FEE. Hazlitt also cites his only novel, *Time Will Run Back* (1966), first published in 1951 as *The Great Idea.*

Hazlitt recounts in this book the tale of the first Thanksgiving when, after "the starving time," the Pilgrims instituted private property ownership, "and instead of famine, now God gave them plentie." The source cited for this story was Hazlitt's *Newsweek* column

(June 27, 1949), based on the account of Plymouth colony's governor William Bradford's *Of Plymouth Plantation: 1620*-1647, first published from the manuscript version in the mid-nineteenth century. Bradford's journal has been republished by Knopf (1952, 1959), McGraw (1981), and Heritage Book (1990). The story of our first Thanksgiving has been retold many times—in FEE's monthly journal, *The Freeman,* as well as elsewhere.

Finally, an interesting sidelight. When working on this book, Hazlitt sent his wife, Frances, to the library to borrow a condensation of the Bible. She found published selections, abridgements of individual books and chapters, but no condensation of the entire Bible. "Why not do one yourself?" he asked. She did, and the result was a condensation of the entire King James Bible, synopsizing every one of the sixty-six books. Frances Kanes Hazlitt's *The Concise Bible: A Condensation* (Henry Regnery, 1962; Liberty Fund, 1976) is an introduction, a handy guide, and a convenient reference tool for the general reader.

This Bibliographical Essay does not presume to be all inclusive; it identifies only the more important works cited by Hazlitt.

B.B.G.

June 1998

Index

(Numbers in parenthesis refer to footnotes)

About The Publisher

Founded in 1946 by Leonard Read, the Foundation for Economic Education (FEE) is committed to enriching people's understanding of the economic and ethical advantages of free markets, private property, and strictly limited government.

FEE's focus on education and what we call "the freedom philosophy" was explained cogently many years ago by Leonard Read:

> We do not tell anyone how to run his life; instead we try to explain how the open market process makes for harmony and peace. We do not look to the political process beyond the bare minimum of protecting life and property; instead we set forth the broad principles that should underlie all law.

The Foundation publishes *The Freeman,* a monthly journal of ideas in the fields of economics, history, and moral philosophy. FEE also publishes books, conducts seminars, distributes op-eds throughout the world, maintains a web site, and sponsors a network of discussion clubs to improve understanding of the principles of a free and prosperous society.

FEE is a nonprofit 501 (c)(3) tax-exempt organization. It is supported only by the contributions of more than 10,000 individuals, businesses, and private foundations.

For further information, please contact:

The Foundation for Economic Education, Inc.
30 South Broadway
Irvington-on-Hudson, NY 10533

Telephone: (914) 591-7230 - Fax: (914) 591-8910
E-mail: freeman@fee.org
FEE Home Page: http://www.fee.org